How To Change Your Hell Into Heaven

Written By: Cathy Ciaramitaro

Endorsements

Death is life's process! For many of us that reality is often overlooked, or at best deeply misunderstood. In this book my friend, Cathy Ciaramitaro, explains this eternal principle that becomes the starting point to engaging a life of continual victory and joy! Through the struggles of her own life to the life-giving power of the cross, Cathy reveals the power of Christ to transform the environment of your life from one of toxic disappointment and blame to a place of celebration and growth. I highly recommend you read this book with a heart wide open and a mind ready for renewal.

Bishop Tony Miller
Destiny World Outreach

This work is timely and with Cathy's usual gifting, she is real, clear (instead of a head jerk for direction, she snaps up an arm with a pointed finger in the right direction) and her stories are so graphic, each one who encounters her work will be clearly blessed.

Thank you Cathy for sharing your thoughts, and insights with such compassion and excellence. God will surely use this message today.

Jim Clark
Apostolic Overseer
B.C.C.N. and Bethany World Prayer Center

Even before Cathy had written her book on the Cross, she had experienced both the pain and the authority of it. Now her desire is to help others as she looks back on her journey and recognizes that He was there every step of the way.

In this powerful and personal book, you will experience the elements that can turn your "hell" into "heaven." Even during the times of great pain and wilderness exposure, you can know the reality of "I will never leave you nor forsake you."

This is a "must read" for anyone wanting to experience the freedom from trauma and pain.

George Woodward
OBFF Board Member

As you read this book, I believe your spirit will be stirred! Cathy has written a practical, yet powerful book to move us from where we are to the place God has for us. As you read this book, I believe the Holy Spirit will empower you to gain a stronger understanding of Jesus' sacrifice, pain and resurrection life.

Pastor Jill Neilson
Bramalea Christian Fellowship

Contents

Forward

I have witnessed, after over thirty years in full time ministry, that many Christians seem to have a wrong image and impression of God. Because of this, it is not uncommon for some to abandon their faith in Christ when they go through tests and trials. Jesus addressed this very issue in the parable of the sower and the seed in the gospels. In Mark's gospel, He said if you don't understand the parable of the sower and the seed you will have difficulty understanding the other parables He taught.

Then Jesus said to them, "If you can't understand the meaning of this parable, how will you understand all the other parables?" Mark 4:13 (NLT) (You can read the entire parable in Mark 4:1–11.)

This book is about the keys to living victoriously and reveals how we can change any circumstance into a blessing when we **STOP AND THINK** about specific things.

I believe that if we know God for His true character and have faith in Him based on that knowledge it will change how we see everything.

Jesus taught that the road that leads to destruction was wide and many would take it, but the road that leads to life is

narrow and *few would find it*. Throughout this book we will
identify which road we are actually on. I pray that you will
understand and desire all that God has for you and how you
can obtain it as you **STOP AND THINK** about the truths
revealed in each chapter in learning how to suffer, die, and
experience resurrection life. It is truth: the truth that Jesus
talked about that will bring to you heaven on earth. Life is
meant for so much more than what this world offers when
you refuse to be deceived, and life brings purpose to embrace
the will of God for your life. He is for us and not against us
and has made a way for hell to be broken from over us!

When someone writes a book they rarely write it alone.
Without the love and support of many it would be a difficult
task. I owe so much to my family and friends, who have been
there for me with their love and support. First and foremost
I want to thank my awesome husband Rick, through whom I
learned many of my life's lessons. He has always been there
for me and pushed me to be all I can be.

I also want to thank my six wonderful *children* and their
spouses, *Melissa* and Shawn, *R.J.* and Mary, *Brian* and Sheri,
Tara and Gary, *Tim* and Steffany and *Jaime* and Jake. I am
proud of every one of them and so thankful to God that they
have grown to be anointed men and women of God. They
have also blessed me with sixteen grandchildren; Joshua,
Trysten, Paris, Zoe, Zachery, Zander and Zane, Isabelle,
Abigail, Tifarah, and Nadiah, Cleah Clara, and Olivia and
Violet and Vince. I truly am a blessed woman!

A special thanks goes to Kelly Penner, my personal

assistant who assisted me whenever possible with this book, serving me and editing faithfully. I greatly appreciate Vince and Terri Pistor for taking the time to edit also and help me through the process. My appreciation goes to Marilyn Czachor who critiqued and edited, as well. Stephanie and Robin, special thanks to you for being there when my lack of computer skills needed your expertise! I couldn't have done it without you all.

There have been so many that God has used in my life to teach me life lessons, and I cannot possibly thank every one of them, but I will say the staff of Windsor Christian Fellowship is amazing.

CHAPTER ONE

THE KEY TO OVERCOMING TEMPTATION

Have you ever had a day from hell? A day where everything goes wrong and then it gets worse? A day when you feel like it is over for you, you can't go on and you just want to curl up in a ball and die? How about the other end of the spectrum when you have the best day of your life, "a pinch me because I think I'm dreaming day"—a day that seemed to drop down from heaven? I believe here on earth, we get a taste of heaven and hell. I have experienced days where I have actually said "This is heaven on earth!" and there have been other occasions where I said, "This is a day from hell."

One such day from heaven was the day I had an amazing experience with the Cross after coming home from seeing the movie *The Passion of the Christ*.

It was on that day that I realized the intensity of the love of God for me; I was totally overwhelmed by it, even though I had been saved for thirty-three years. It took me to a whole new level of joy and awe in my relationship with Christ. That experience also launched me into a richer and deeper dimension of what God had called me to, as an incredible new passion for the Cross was birthed inside of me.

A day from hell was on January 9th, 1988—the day I came home from shopping with some friends to find out my husband had died in a car wreck. That day thrust me unexpectedly into a difficult road of suffering that I was forced to walk through. Overwhelming grief, pain, and difficulty enveloped me in a cloud of darkness like I had never before experienced. I had to battle daily to go on and keep myself from drowning in its grip of despair. It felt like hell.

We have all had those amazing days, and those days that seemed to come from the pit of hell. God Himself knows what it's like to experience all that life throws at us. Jesus went through hell on earth to gain heaven for us and to show us how to receive His promises here in this life. I believe that changing our hell into heaven is determined by the choices we make when we feel engulfed in the flames of discouragement, disappointment, hopelessness, and heartache. There is a way out; there is a better day, but we have to position ourselves to get there. Romans 14:7–9 says:

> *7. For we don't live for ourselves or die for ourselves. 8. If we live, it's to honor the Lord. And if we die, it's to honor the Lord. So whether we live or die, we belong to the Lord. 9. Christ died and rose again for this very purpose—to be Lord of the living and the dead.*

The Bible tells us that the Kingdom of God is not simply a place, but it is here among us now (as *a state of being*) as we can read in the following scriptures.

> *For the Kingdom of God is not just a lot of talk; it is living by God's power. Which do you choose? Should I come with a rod to punish you, or should I come with love and a gentle spirit?* 1 Corinthians 4:20–21 (NLT):

To receive the promises of God's Kingdom, we must let go of our old life; die to living for ourselves, and surrender to His Lordship. When we go to a new country or kingdom it is important that we know the laws in that kingdom. Recently, I was in the United Kingdom, and I rented a car. I made my way onto the highway, driving on the opposite side of the road from what I was accustomed to. I checked for speed limit signs and discovering that there weren't any, I went as fast as I felt I could. Unfortunately I was speeding and a month later I received four speeding tickets. I was unaware that the highway was under camera surveillance. I felt it was unfair that the speed was not posted; however, ultimately I was responsible to know the law. Ignorance of the law is no excuse, and therefore I had to pay the fines. Every kingdom has its laws of operation, as does God's. We are responsible to know that His Kingdom operates by the principle of dying to our selfish nature. Dying to our selfishness requires an element of suffering, and no one wants to suffer. Though it is often difficult and at times painful, we wrestle with whether or not to surrender fully to Him. Obedience is necessary to change our hell into heaven. Every time we die to self we solidify the decision to serve Him with our whole heart which results in victorious eternal life. To suffer and die in order to obtain life is the only sure way to bring us the true blessings of God. This is the Key Kingdom Principle of how we can change our hell into heaven, and it works! I really like a following quote from A.W. Tozer book "The Radical Cross" – Living the Passion of Christ.

"The whole question of right and wrong, of moral responsibility, of justice and judgment and reward and punishment, is sharply accented for us by the fact that we are members of a fallen race, occupying a position halfway between hell and heaven, with the knowledge of good and evil inherent within our intricate natures, along with ability to turn toward good and an inborn propensity to turn toward evil."

Now before you throw this book down, dreading another message on suffering and sacrifice, remember . . . you WILL suffer, it's just how, when, and why. Don't be an itching ear, cafeteria-style Christian who picks and chooses only what appeals to your flesh from God's Word. Tough it up, refuse to be deceived, and find out how to get what you really want out of life.

Jesus talked about this in Matthew as we can read here:

> *39 If you cling to your life, you will lose it; but if you give up your life for me, you will find it.* Matthew 10:38–39 (NLT)

It is amazing to know that God created the world and everything in it; but even more amazing, is the fact that He left us instructions on how to live successfully. Not only did He leave us with instructions, but He Himself came and demonstrated them for us

God is good, holy, just, loving and righteous. We are not. He lives by principles, and eternal ones at that. Ultimately, to Him, it is all about having character that lives by those principles. Living outside of His principles leaves you on a path of defeat, failure, and great loss. It's plain and simple, yet so many believers fail to see it. The way to live out these principles for an overcoming victorious life was demonstrated incredibly through the life and death of Jesus Christ. The Cross is the ultimate expression of how those principles actually work, and when we see this we will find victory in every aspect of our lives.

The keys to living an overcoming life that will keep you in righteousness peace, and joy are simple and liberating. They are not necessarily easy to walk out, but definitely possible if you follow the steps I will be sharing.

Throughout this book I am going to refer often to three words that describe the steps to victory, which will result in changing your hell into heaven. The three words are SUFFER, DIE, and LIFE. Without going through suffering and death in the choices we make every day we will never experience real life and victory. Of course we will not have to suffer and die for our sins; that is a free gift from God, but Jesus taught us that to gain our life we must lose it.

Before I continue, I want to clarify that the suffering I am referring to is not God's punishment; but rather the battle we go through every time we wrestle with our fleshly desires when endeavoring to obey God. As long as we live in our natural body, our fleshly desires will be in conflict with being led by the Spirit. In every circumstance life throws at us, our flesh wants to do the opposite of what will change our hell into heaven and instead desires to do what keeps us trapped in hell's grip. We can read about this conflict in Romans 8.

> *5 Those who are dominated by the sinful nature think about sinful things, but those who are controlled by the Holy Spirit think about things that please the Spirit. 6 So letting your sinful nature control your mind leads to death. But letting the Spirit control your mind leads to life and peace.* Romans 8:5–6 (NLT)

It is very clear in this portion of scripture that we must share in His suffering to share in His Glory. Our flesh suffers every time we battle temptation. The key to gaining victory over our flesh involves what we ***think about***. We can either think about what our flesh wants, or we can think about things that please the Spirit.

An example of this principle that I personally experience is when I am feeling hurt by my husband because he may not be as sensitive to me as I think he should be when I am under a lot of stress. This happens often when we are about to do some entertaining. I expect him to do certain things, and I start making demands on him that he doesn't always get to or he doesn't do it to my standards. Because my home has to look perfect when I have company, I can get very upset if things don't get done exactly the way I want them to. As a result my flesh wants to say or do something to let him know that I disapprove of him or his performance. If I take a moment and stop and think about Christ, and what He went through for me, it will put the moment into perspective and I will quickly realize that my temptation to hurt my husband is really something I should die to. My flesh doesn't like it, it wants to complain. However the benefit for my marriage, by holding my tongue or better yet affirming what he does do for me, is far more important than expressing my discontent and disappointment. One of my favorite passages of scripture that explains this is in Hebrews 12.

> *1 Therefore, since we are surrounded by such a huge crowd of witnesses to the life of faith, let us strip off every weight that slows us down, especially the sin that so easily trips us up. And let us run with endurance the race God has set before us. 2 We do this by keeping our eyes on Jesus, the champion who initiates and perfects our faith. Because of the joy awaiting him, he endured the cross, disregarding its shame. Now he is seated in the place of honor beside God's throne. 3 Think of all the hostility he endured from sinful people; then you won't become weary and give up. 4 After all, you have not yet given your lives in your struggle against sin. Hebrew 12:1–4 (NLT)*

When we CHOOSE to THINK ABOUT the things Jesus endured when He suffered and died, we will be empowered to make the right choices of obedience to God. Otherwise it is impossible to do on our own. Jesus was able to endure His suffering by thinking about the JOY awaiting Him on the other side of the cross. THIS IS THE KEY PRINCIPLE TO LIVING KINGDOM LIFE AND ENABLING YOU TO CHANGE YOUR HELL INTO HEAVEN!

Every time you overcome temptation (suffer) and die, life is produced in you and you move forward on your journey to success.

Of course we know that Jesus suffered, died, and rose again to save us from our sins, and that the greatest gift to us is the gift of salvation. To be forgiven and reconciled to God is something we should not take for granted but be thankful for every day of our lives. However the Cross was not only for the purpose of salvation but also a physical demonstration of the *keys to victory* in every aspect of our lives.

If Jesus's death on the Cross was only for our forgiveness of sins then he would have died in the same manner that the Jewish High Priests killed the animals they sacrificed for the sins of the nation of Israel. When they slaughtered the animal they would slit its throat with a sharp knife, and it would die a quick and easy death. They did not torture it first.

Jesus could have died that way and still be the sacrificial lamb that died for our sins, but He didn't choose that type of death. He chose to be beaten, tortured, shamed, and humiliated in every way. There were 2 main reasons for this. The first we can read about in Isaiah.

> *4 Yet it was our weaknesses he carried; it was our sorrows that weighed him down. And we thought his troubles were a punishment from God, a punishment for his own sins.* Isaiah 53:4 (NLT)

Here we can see that he carried every sorrow known to man, along with the pain and humiliation of all of our sins. God wanted to identify and connect with us so that when we go to Him we can have assurance that He understands us in every way.

My book *The Cross* focuses on the first reason which brings inner healing to the pain you have experienced in your life. Whether you have been betrayed, abandoned, beaten, falsely accused, shamed, or left on a road of suffering; God went to that place. He experienced your pain and connects with you in your pain to give you hope and healing for a better day. Victory is always ahead when you trust Him in your trial.

This book is about the second reason; *Overcoming temptation*. OVERCOMING TEMPTATION can be like GOING THROUGH HELL TO GAIN HEAVEN.

Jesus subjected himself to horrific torture and pain of every kind not only to identify with all human suffering and heal us from it, but to also show us how to overcome the temptations we face, whether big or small.

Overcoming temptations is the key to experiencing heaven on earth because we will suffer in this life regardless. It's just a matter of whether we choose our suffering or become a victim of it. That is why it is so important that we get this. When we understand the principle of SUFFER, DIE, and LIFE, we will suffer a lot less and experience great joy and blessing in our lives. Yes, we may have to go through some hell to gain heaven; but if we try to bypass the process and live selfishly by following our fleshly desires, we will experience hell on earth in the long run and never benefit from the life God created us for.

In the following chapters I will cover the key areas Christ spoke about in the last hours of His life. In His dying words, He revealed that we are called to establish His Kingdom through suffering and dying in order to produce true life. It was those words that positioned Him for resurrection life and that show us how to change our hell into heaven.

Application to **CHANGE YOUR HELL INTO HEAVEN**.

Read and meditate on Hebrews 12:1–4
Hebrew 12:1–4

> *1 Therefore, since we are surrounded by such a huge crowd of witnesses to the life of faith, let us strip off every weight that slows us down, especially the sin that so easily trips us up. And let us run with endurance the race God has set before us. 2 We do this by*

keeping our eyes on Jesus, the champion who initiates and perfects our faith. Because of the joy awaiting him, he endured the cross, disregarding its shame. Now he is seated in the place of honor beside God's throne. 3 Think of all the hostility he endured from sinful people; then you won't become weary and give up. 4 After all, you have not yet given your lives in your struggle against sin.

Take a few moments and **STOP AND THINK** *about the suffering Jesus went through for us that led to His resurrection. I mean really think about it!* Without His willingness to die to selfishness, there would be no resurrection life. The key to changing our hell into heaven is to know that we must *choose to suffer and die to self to gain the life on the other side of our trial.*

CHAPTER TWO

IN THE VALLEY OF DECISION

~✍

Have you ever made a decision when faced with temptation that you deeply regretted? When I think back over my life my biggest regrets are the reckless things I did as a rebellious teenager. I regret running away from home at fourteen years of age, breaking my mother's heart and giving her several years of fear and worry for my well-being. At that time I went for months without even calling her to let her know I was okay. Now as a mother I realize what I must have put her through. I also regret abusing my body with the use of illegal drugs. Later in life as a mother I wish I had spent more time with my children, treasuring the time I had them at home. I also regret words I have spoken and choices I have made in spending money. I can't tell you how many times I regret eating some delectable food, especially when I stood on the scale. Unfortunately you cannot go back and change what you have already done, but you can choose what you will do today.

Every day we are faced with decisions, big and small. Regardless of the size, they all come with CONSEQUENCES that will show up in our lives: whether now or later, they will show up. The decisions we make affect our relationships, health, productivity, wealth, character, worship, and eternal destiny. These choices are the sum total of who we are and what we get out of life.

If you don't like the person you've become or where you are at in your life, God gives you options that WILL change how you see everything about yourself and your circumstances. These options if heeded change everything about you. To get what you really want out of life you have to make the choices that will get you there. This involves doing God's will and not your own. Doing God's will requires something from you because God is concerned about one thing in you. HE IS PRIMARILY CONCERNED ABOUT THE CONDITION OF YOUR HEART. Nothing matters more to Him. Whatever is in your heart will eventually determine your choices, and what you choose will determine the course of your life. We can read about this in Proverbs.

> *Guard your heart above all else, for it determines the course of your life.* Proverbs 4:23 (NLT)

He wants your heart to be like Christ's in obedience to Him so that He can impart all of His riches, benefits, and power into your life. This involves the suffering and death to selfishness so that, His amazing life can overtake you.

The first place where we must surrender is in the area of receiving the gift of salvation by repenting of our sins, believing in Jesus Christ, and getting baptized.

It starts with obedience. Doing this means that the very Spirit of Christ now lives in you to empower you to live your life as Christ did. This involves knowing *how* Jesus dealt with temptation. The act of baptism is a symbol of dying to self to live a new life for God. One of the greatest tests of temptation and suffering Jesus experienced took place not on the cross, but in the Garden of Gethsemane.

> *39 Then, accompanied by the disciples, Jesus left the upstairs room and went as usual to the Mount of Olives. 40 There he told them, "Pray that you will not give in to temptation." 41 He walked away, about a stone's throw, and knelt down and prayed, 42 "Father, if you are willing, please take this cup of suffering away from me. Yet I want your will to be done, not mine." 43 Then an angel from heaven appeared and strengthened him. 44 He prayed more fervently, and he was in such agony of spirit that his sweat fell to the ground like great drops of blood." 45 At last he stood up again and returned to the disciples, only to find them asleep, exhausted from grief. 46 "Why are you sleeping?" he asked them. "Get up and pray, so that you will not give in to temptation."*
> Luke 22:39–46 (NLT)

This passage of scripture demonstrates the suffering and agony that transpires in the heart of temptation. Jesus was clearly wrestling with his flesh which was seeking another way that he could do the Father's will for Him. The Father's will was that he would bear the sins of the world, paying the full penalty and having the full wrath of God poured out on him. Torture and death on the Cross was his path to the life on the other side. He couldn't get the life without the suffering and death first. It was here Jesus suffered the greatest in the valley of decision. It was in that place that he made the choice to die to his flesh and do the right thing, regardless of the cost to himself. This is the true test of humility and obedience, that revealed what was in His heart: **HUMILITY.**

The result for Jesus obeying His Father caused His suffering and death on the Cross, but the final outcome was resurrection life. He went to the lowest place—the most humble place—to get to the highest place, and now he possesses a Name above every name.

How did Jesus do it? He didn't leave us clueless but told us several things in this passage of scripture that will give us the power to overcome temptation. The first is PRAY that you will not give into the temptation. This in itself requires suffering and death in us. To pray we often wrestle with our flesh to do something else. Distractions are everywhere. The excuses are abundant. In our modern culture we are so busy with things such as Facebook, twitter, email, and countless apps that cry for our time.

Because my Bibles are in my iPad along with all my social media, there is a strong temptation for me to check my email, twitter, or Facebook while I am trying to spend time with God. Prayer itself requires dying to the things that would keep us from the throne of God. However, when we choose to refuse to give into all the reasons not to pray and boldly enter into the presence of God in prayer we die to self and life is produced in us. Prayer is the true place of humility, knowing we need God and seeking His help in our lives. But in that place of prayer we are faced with a choice, as we can see in the words of Jesus. Prayer is the place where we are empowered to change our hell into heaven.

The second thing Jesus said in the garden was "not my will but yours be done." This is really the seat of all temptation. Every temptation is faced with this choice, our will or His. *Not my will but yours* is the greatest destroyer of our pride, which is the root of sin that comes straight from Satan himself. Satan fell because of his pride, and he is the author of it. Eve fell because of her pride; therefore the seed of pride coming from Satan was birthed in fallen man. Submitting to God destroys that seed in us. Our pride doesn't want to go down easy; therefore we suffer in the process. Conversely, when we die to it there is freedom and joy!

I recall many times when I really didn't want to do something that God was asking me to do. My flesh did not want to obey, and I tried to come up with every excuse I could think of to get out of it. One such time was when God asked me to spend time with a girl I really didn't like because she was always negative and complained about everything. God had asked me to have her over for lunch and the thought of it really upset me. I tried to justify my disobedience, but finally I gave in to what God was asking me to do. That lunch turned out to be a huge learning curve for me, as I asked this seemingly undesirable person to tell me about her life. As I listened intently, she told one the most heart wrenching stories of abuse and suffering I have ever heard. Her mother had died shortly after she was born. She was raised by her father who verbally, sexually, and physically abused her during her entire childhood. This left her with several physical and mental disabilities that continually brought her rejection, even in the church. As a child she was kept in a cabin in the wilderness subject to this horrible abuse and wasn't discovered until she was twelve years old. My heart wept as her story unfolded, and God revealed to me how much He wanted to demonstrate His love to her through His body, the church. I, like so many others, had been judgmental and rejected her, not realizing the deep need inside of her to be loved and accepted. This powerful lesson changed my life. Obeying God enriched me and gave life to someone else in desperate need. Jesus talked about this in his great temptations while fasting in the desert as we can read here in Matthew.

> *1 Then Jesus was led by the Spirit into the wilderness to be tempted there by the devil. 2 For forty days and forty nights he fasted and became very hungry. 3 During that time the devil came and said to him, "If you are the Son*

of God, tell these stones to become loaves of bread. But Jesus told him, "No! The Scriptures say, 'People do not live by bread alone, but by every word that comes from the mouth of God.' " 5 Then the devil took him to the holy city, Jerusalem, to the highest point of the Temple, 6 and said, "If you are the Son of God, jump off! For the Scriptures say, 'He will order his angels to protect you. And they will hold you up with their hands so you won't even hurt your foot on a stone.' " 7 Jesus responded, "The Scriptures also say, 'You must not test the LORD your God.' "
8 Next the devil took him to the peak of a very high mountain and showed him all the kingdoms of the world and their glory. 9 "I will give it all to you," he said, "if you will kneel down and worship me." 10 "Get out of here, Satan," Jesus told him. "For the Scriptures say, 'You must worship the LORD your God and serve only him.' " 11 Then the devil went away, and angels came and took care of Jesus.
Matthew 4 (NLT)

It is here he said three things that gave him victory over his flesh.

1. We must live by every word that comes from God.

2. We must not test God.

3. We must worship and serve Him alone.

Most of us serve and trust ourselves more than we do God, which is the spirit of pride. Pride is in opposition to

God's Kingdom which operates by humility. One kingdom is of Satan, the other of God. God Himself is humble. When Jesus Christ subjected Himself to the shame and indignities of the Cross He proved that. In Hebrews we can read how Christ revealed the exact character of God.

The Son radiates God's own glory and expresses the very character of God, and he sustains everything by the mighty power of his command. When he had cleansed us from our sins, he sat down in the place of honor at the right hand of the majestic God in heaven. Hebrews 1: 3 (NLT)

When we humble ourselves we become more like God, and we experience some suffering (not getting the accolades we want) because our flesh desires to be exalted. When we choose His will in spite of what our flesh desires, we die to the kingdom of this world and inherit the life of His kingdom. It is then we experience amazing, abundant, and powerful life that releases true love, joy, and peace — and inwardly our hell is transformed into heaven.

Because we are still in our flesh, temptations seem relentless as our pride, and fleshly desires don't die easily. In fact, it seems that with each victory another battle looms around the corner. We will wrestle in the valley of decision every day of our lives, which is why we must die daily. We are constantly confronted with the choices of our will versus God's. It is these choices that determine how much of heaven or hell we will experience.

Our example is Christ Jesus. He made the way for us to overcome our flesh.

Jesus not only demonstrated how to overcome our flesh but spoke from the Cross about the areas that we are to suffer and die in to gain life. He left nothing uncovered! It amazes me that the cross speaks for all eternity and its message is so profound. We must have eyes to see it and be willing to embrace its truth. When we do, we will experience the Kingdom of Heaven now!

Application to **CHANGE YOUR HELL INTO HEAVEN**

Read and meditate on Proverbs 4:23

> *Guard your heart above all else, for it determines the course of your life.* Proverbs 4:23 (NLT)

STOP AND THINK that whatever we choose to do will be a witness (good or bad) to the people we influence; therefore *choose the path of humility by obedience to God. This will position us to experience heaven on earth and be richly blessed by God!*

CHAPTER THREE

DYING TO FORGIVE

❧

On October 2, 2006, a shooting occurred at a one room Amish School at the West Nickel Mines in the Township of Lancaster County, Pennsylvania. The gunman, Charles Carl Roberts IV, who was not Amish, the local milkman for that community, entered the school and ordered the girls (aged 6–13) to line up against the chalkboard and shot ten of them, killing five. A Roberts family spokesman said an Amish neighbor comforted the Roberts family hours after the shooting and extended forgiveness to them. Amish community members visited and comforted Roberts' widow, parents, and parents-in-law. The Amish also set up a charitable fund for the family of the shooter, and 30 of them attended his funeral. Marie Roberts, the widow of the killer, was one of the few outsiders invited to the funeral of one of the victims. Marie Roberts wrote an open letter to her Amish neighbors thanking them for their forgiveness, grace, and mercy. [1]

---

[1] Details taken from Wikipedia under "Amish School Shooting"

Unforgiveness is like a prison that holds its captives in tormenting bondage, but forgiveness is powerful. Willingness to forgive breaks the chains from your life. I recently heard a quote from Chip Ingram stating that "holding onto unforgiveness is like drinking poison and expecting the other person to die."

The first thing Jesus cried out from the cross was *"Father forgive them they know not what they do."* I can't imagine the suffering Jesus endured as he called out these powerful words. At the height of His injustice, humiliation, and pain His words sent His message for all of eternity to all who will hear. Just to speak them emanated His willingness to suffer and die for us, but they weren't only spoken to forgive us but to show us where we too must start in our suffering and dying to self.

When we are hurt by someone our flesh, or selfish and prideful nature, rises up and wants to hurt back. We want to make them pay and suffer like they did to us. Jesus taught that unforgiveness reveals that we are in pride and shuts the door on being forgiven ourselves. We can read about this in Matthew 18.

> *23 "Therefore, the Kingdom of Heaven can be compared to a king who decided to bring his accounts up to date with servants who had borrowed money from him. 24 In the process, one of his debtors was brought in who owed him millions of dollars. 25 He couldn't pay, so his master ordered that he be sold—along with his wife, his children, 26 but the man fell down*

before his master and begged him, 'Please, be patient with me, and I will pay it all.' 27 Then his master was filled with pity for him, and he released him and forgave his debt. 28 "But when the man left the king, he went to a fellow servant who owed him a few thousand dollars. He grabbed him by the throat and demanded instant payment. 29 "His fellow servant fell down before him and begged for a little more time. 'Be patient with me, and I will pay it,' he pleaded. 30 But his creditor wouldn't wait. He had the man arrested and put in prison until the debt could be paid in full. 31 "When some of the other servants saw this, they were very upset. They went to the king and told him everything that had happened. 32 Then the king called in the man he had forgiven and said, 'You evil servant! I forgave you that tremendous debt because you pleaded with me. 33 Shouldn't you have mercy on your fellow servant, just as I had mercy on you?' 34 Then the angry king sent the man to prison to be tortured until he had paid his entire debt and everything he owned—to pay the debt. Matthew 18:23–34 (NLT)

Basically what Jesus is referring to in this passage of scripture is when we have been forgiven by God for a lifetime of sin, we have the audacity to hold people's sins against them. The evil he refers to in this story, is PRIDE. "How dare they hurt me!" bombards our carnal thinking, as we so easily forget the amazing grace and forgiveness that has been freely extended to us from the Cross. Our flesh wants our offenders to pay in full, yet we want to be forgiven and go free. Who do we think we are? The answer is found in our selfishness and pride.

Jesus gives us many great promises in His Word, but there are conditions with them. One of the key conditions is to forgive others. In fact God WILL NOT FORGIVE US if we don't forgive others as we can read here in Mark.

> *22 Then Jesus said to the disciples, "Have faith in God. 23 I tell you the truth, you can say to this mountain, "May you be lifted up and thrown into the sea," and it will happen. But you must really believe it will happen and have no doubt in your heart. 24 I tell you, you can pray for anything, and if you believe that you've received it, it will be yours. 25 But when you are praying, first forgive anyone you are holding a grudge against, so that your Father in heaven will forgive your sins, too."*
> *Mark 11:22–25 (NLT)*

Notice that in verse 25 it says SO THAT YOUR FATHER IN HEAVEN WILL FORGIVE YOU! There is a condition for receiving what you ask for in faith. It gives our flesh great satisfaction when we can cause suffering to someone who has disappointed or harmed us in some way. This is one of the biggest reasons families are torn apart. Unforgiveness rears its ugly head in our closest relationships especially our marriages.

As I shared earlier, I often used to make my husband suffer when he didn't meet up to my expectation in some way. One way I would do this was to give him the silent treatment. This really pleased my flesh and I savored his concern when he knew something was wrong between us. I entertained all the thoughts of everything he had ever done that upset me and how he deserved the treatment I was giving him. I wanted him to figure out where he had let me down and make it right, and I was going to make sure he paid until he did. I thought I was gaining an advantage but really I was losing. What I really wanted was a great marriage, but my resentment and desire to make him pay continually ate away at the strength of our relationship. Instead of the life I wanted, death was being produced. Hurting him was slowly destroying our marriage because unforgiveness was at the helm of my heart. The root of unforgiveness was my pride.

God demands humility, but our flesh is all about exalting ourselves. Pride kept me from what I wanted, a great marriage. My resentment only built barriers in our relationship that produced hell on earth. If pleasing our flesh is not the answer, what is? Jesus cried out the answer from the Cross. *"Father forgive them they know not what they do!"* This was a demonstration of His character and His willingness to forgive us, in spite of how much we hurt and disappoint Him!

Every time we are offended, or upset with someone we are faced with the decision of His will or ours. This is where we get to choose to suffer and have an opportunity to change our hell into heaven or stay in hell. Do we heed the voice of God or our flesh? Do we suffer now, or suffer later?

Forgiveness does not mean we don't confront and deal with issues that should be addressed. However, when we do have to confront, we do so with humility and love, not anger, pride, and hatred. Consequences may have to be implemented for serious offenses, but how they are implemented is important. Consequences when necessary are good for the offenders and help them change destructive behaviour that hurts themselves as well as others. Ultimately proper consequences can result in BLESSING the person hurting us in the long run but we must remember that *many offenses are minor and should be overlooked*. Seeking God and being led by His Spirit will guide us to evaluate each situation and how to respond. Too often we major on minors, and enable what is major. Serious issues of offense should not be ignored, but dealt with in a spirit of forgiveness and humility.

Regardless of the offense, resentment, bitterness, and revenge are the fleshly desires we must die to in order to break the chains of hell from our hearts and minds. We can choose to perpetuate a life of hell on earth or walk in freedom, peace, and love. Forgiving someone liberates us, blesses us, and brings that life of power and freedom. Every time we refuse to obey the thoughts that motivate us to hurt the one who hurt us, we die to our pride. When we choose humility we are choosing life, and this pleases God. It is then that God wins, we win, and Satan loses. Just think of the freedom we can walk in when we set someone else free by forgiving them!

Now is the time to bring those who have hurt or offended us to the foot of the cross. We must release them of their sin so that we can be forgiven knowing that Jesus Christ died to forgive them too. Change your hell into heaven by letting go of the hated anger and bitterness that holds you in hell's grip. Humble yourself before a merciful loving God and be forgiven and extend forgiveness. It is heaven on earth!

Even though we may still feel hurt, as we connect with Jesus and see His willingness to forgive us from the Cross for every sin we've ever committed, we will be overwhelmed with gratitude for His love and mercy for us. This transforms our perspective and our heart, producing great joy and humility in us, making it easier to forgive our offender. Healing begins at the cross. The transgressions of others will no longer hold us in their deadly grip keeping us in bondage. The truth will set us free, and freedom is heaven on earth.

Holding on to offense is choosing to be chained to Satan. Choosing to walk in forgiveness is choosing to live in God's Kingdom. Don't let Satan, the god of this world, keep you captive any longer in a living hell but instead die to unforgiveness and find true life. Choose to change your hell into heaven.

Application to **CHANGE YOUR HELL INTO HEAVEN**

Read and meditate on Mark 11:22–25

> *22 Then Jesus said to the disciples, "Have faith in God. 23 I tell you the truth, you can say to this mountain, 'May you be lifted up and thrown into the sea,' and it will happen. But you must really believe it will happen and*

have no doubt in your heart. 24 I tell you, you can pray for anything, and if you believe that you've received it, it will be yours. 25 But when you are praying, first forgive anyone you are holding a grudge against, so that your Father in heaven will forgive your sins, too." Mark 11:22–25 (NLT)*

STOP AND THINK about the lifetime of sins we have been forgiven of; ponder every evil thing you have ever done that He has graciously pardoned and taken from you. *Doing this changes our perspective. It gives us appreciation for God's great mercy and empowering us to forgive those that have hurt us. The chains of bondage are broken from our lives freeing us from bitterness and unforgiveness.*

CHAPTER FOUR

DYING FOR A KILLER

Jesus was mocked and jeered at as he hung on the cross, yet in the height of his humiliation and torture he thought of others over himself. On either side of him were two thieves, dying on crosses because of their crimes. One of them saw something beyond the natural circumstance and called out to Him for salvation. Jesus was in the same predicament; he was suffering and helpless at the hands of an angry mob yet he was a witness, a light in the darkness, demonstrating the character of God himself. With agonizing breath, he uttered these words *"Today you will be with me in paradise,"* which we can read here in Luke.

> *39 One of the criminals hanging beside him scoffed, "So you're the Messiah, are you? Prove it by saving yourself—and us, too, while you're at it!" 40 But the other criminal protested, "Don't you fear God even when you have been sentenced to die? 41 We deserve to die for our crimes, but this man hasn't done anything wrong." 42 Then he*

*said, "Jesus, remember me when you come
into your Kingdom." 43 And Jesus replied,
"I assure you, today you will be with me in
paradise."* Luke 23:39–43

In spite of his shame and humiliation he gave hope to
another hurting person. Being a witness for the Kingdom of
God requires sacrifice and selflessness. It involves forget-
ting about your own desires, comforts and reputation and
meeting the needs of another by dying to self.

There are many days when I am tired, frustrated, or
feeling sorry for myself and allow those feelings to be an
excuse to ignore the opportunities to ease the hurt of a fellow
human being.

We as believers need to realize that we really are the
temples of the living Holy Spirit of God, the creator of heaven
and earth. He has given us His Spirit to lead and guide us and
to demonstrate the love of God to a lost and broken world.
As his children it is no longer about us, but others. We are to
be a light and a voice to give hope where there is none. There
are needy people everywhere just waiting for God's love to
be demonstrated to them. Jesus was all about meeting needs
and He saw how much needed to be done. We can read here
in Matthew that He wanted prayer for more workers!

*37 He said to his disciples, "The harvest is
great, but the workers are few. 18 So pray
to the Lord who is in charge of the harvest;
ask him to send more workers into his fields.*
Matt 9:37–38 (NLT)

That word is still true today but unfortunately there are too few people heeding the call.

Years ago I was blessed to be friends with a precious widow named Myra*. Myra loved Jesus and had little concern for herself. Living alone and on a fixed income she was radiant with the joy of the Lord. At the time I knew her, we were members of the same small church. It was also at that time when several young women were brutally raped and murdered in our city in Ontario. There was great fear as a serial killer was on the loose, and the murders became major news across Canada. Several months after the crimes began; the killer was caught when his latest victim lived after being left for dead and was able to identify him. Of course, the subsequent trial was highly publicized and aired nationwide. Many Canadians were following the trial on a daily basis, fixed on their desire to see justice done and see this monster pay for his hideous crimes. Myra saw something else. One day as she was glued to the trial on TV, she saw the face of the killer's wife, Katie*, devastated by her husband's secret life. Myra saw a wife and mother tormented in grief and betrayal by the horrors committed at her husband's hands. Moved with compassion, Myra decided to go down to the courthouse, find this broken woman, and reach out to help her and talk to her about the love of Jesus.

The following day she did just that, and invited Katie to lunch. Katie was shocked that anyone would want to have anything to do with her as her humiliation and shame permeated her to the core. She was married to one of the most hated, despicable men alive at that time and cowered under the judgement of the masses. Her children were also ridiculed, bullied, and hated for the crimes of their father. They too were innocent victims of his demonic choices and were paying the price for it. But Myra showered them with love and support, invited them to our church and led them to the Lord. Our church rallied around Katie and her children, praying for them and helping with the mounting expenses of being left without substantial income. We became their life support while they were drowning in a sea of despair. Soon hope and joy began the healing process as the body of Christ did what we were created to do: the work of his ministry.

Eventually our pastor went to visit Katie's husband in prison and led him to Christ. Remember Jesus even died for rapists and murderers. The good news was that the church was answering the prayer of Jesus for more workers for the vast harvest waiting to be helped.

At that time I was going through my own personal hell and was financially strapped and struggling to get by. But Myra taught me a valuable lesson: focus on others and your hell will become heaven. Joy and love will cause you to rise above whatever difficulty you may be facing, and the power of God will be activated to bring you victory. I remembered this, when my late husband died. While going through the most difficult time of my life, struggling to get up in the morning and wishing I too could die, I found the secret of the Kingdom. At first I had to force myself to focus on others as it took every effort of my will to forget about my pain and focus on someone else's. My flesh wanted to crawl in a hole, lash out in anger; have pity parties, and walk away from my responsibilities, but I knew that would lead to my death. I had to die to myself to gain my breakthrough. Sometimes we have to make a decision to do something regardless of our feelings and the cost to us. I know that I would not be where I am today had I not forced myself to take steps every day when I was hurting and do things that would benefit others.

We are all sinners, condemned to eternal punishment if we don't find forgiveness at the Cross. Forgiveness and healing are extended from the Cross for all, at all times. Our job is to tell those that we are able to influence with this amazing life-changing message, by sharing what God has done. Our personal testimony is our story of God's power and influence in our lives and our actions are verification of this. The Bible says we are being read by all men.

> *You are our epistle written in our hearts , known and read by all men ; 3 clearly you are an epistle of Christ , ministered by us , written not with ink but by the Spirit of the living God , not on tablets of stone but on tablets of flesh , that is, of the heart.*
> 2 Cor. 3:2-3 (NLT)

Recently, I hosted the widows of our church at my home for a time of fellowship. I had them all share what makes them happy, what makes them sad, and what they dream about. As we went around the room, hearing the stories, joys and sorrows of each one, I was overwhelmingly blessed by the ones that exuded great joy and were genuinely fulfilled. They were all woman that I knew lived for others. They were givers, prayer warriors, and were always looking for opportunities to meet needs. The women that were still overcome with grief and sorrow were still very self-focused. They were stuck in their hell while the others had discovered the key to changing their hell into heaven. Obviously, most of the hurting widows were new to their Christian faith and had not yet discovered the key to their freedom. Unfortunately a few had been saved for years but were blinded by self. They lacked peace and joy, and their lives really were depressing because they were feeding their pain by not yet dying to self and becoming the witness they were called to be.

We are all called to be a Godly example, but to do so we must overcome our flesh which constantly gives us excuses that stop us.

I'm too tired, I'm afraid, what if I'm rejected, I'm too busy... the list is endless. Jesus wasn't in the best of circumstances when he gave hope to a dying criminal. I'm sure he could have used his suffering as an excuse to ignore the need of another, but His suffering was for others and that thief was a first fruit of what He was dying for.

Opportunities are all around us, and if we are led by the Spirit we will see them. Jesus said the harvest is plentiful, meaning there is an abundance of people just waiting to hear the Good News, but he also said the labourers are few.

There are few because it costs us something to witness. It may cost us our reputation, some relationships, time, or money, but the rewards are endless. To be a witness we must suffer by laying down what others think of us or what it may cost us. Our flesh will fight the Spirit on this, but when we choose to overcome and witness regardless of what happens to us we die to the flesh and begin to walk in the realm of the supernatural. It is there that God's power will flow freely in our lives. Do we want to live in fear or in unlimited power? We get to choose, but to get life we must suffer and die to self. If we focus on the reward as Jesus did, we will be able to overcome our flesh.

As we choose to be a witness for Christ we will open a powerful door into the realm of God's Kingdom, and we will begin to experience His supernatural power in ways that will bless us and strengthen our faith. We may suffer some rejection or even ridicule, but God will have the final say and use us to reach those crying out for help. Remember the harvest is plentiful. We are God's hands, feet, and voice. Obey Him and He will cause rivers of living water to flow from us bringing life into others. Our hell will be changed into heaven.

*Names have been changed

Application to CHANGE YOUR HELL INTO HEAVEN

Read and meditate on 2 Corinthians 3:2-3

*2 You are our epistle written in our hearts ,
known and read by all men ; 3 clearly you are*

47

*an epistle of Christ , ministered by us , written
not with ink but by the Spirit of the living God
, not on tablets of stone but on tablets of flesh
, that is, of the heart. 2 Cor. 3:2 (NLT)*

STOP AND THINK *of the many hurting and lost people
that need hope and turn from your problems to focus on
helping them.* Doing this will help you realize how blessed
you really are. Focusing on yourself breeds dissatisfaction,
while blessing others brings great joy in your life.

CHAPTER FIVE

HEAVEN IN YOUR HOME

One of my earliest memories was at the age of five. It was the day my father was taken away from us by the police. I have foggy recollections of domestic abuse in our home for the months prior as my father gave into his demons. He was an alcoholic and compulsive gambler and often went into fits of rage that caused us to hide in fear. On this particular day a fight ensued, and I remember hiding behind a door with my younger brother and sister until the police arrived and took him. That was the last time I saw him as a child. Not having a father for most of my childhood had a major negative impact on my life. Rejection, shame, and feelings of insecurity plagued me for years. Only the understanding of the Cross truly set me free from these paralyzing mind sets.

Do you know God is all about family? In fact, the family was His plan, and He had much to say about it. Being part of a family requires something from each of us. Every family member bears some responsibility based on their age and role. Unfortunately today families are falling apart because our flesh wants to avoid responsibility and seeks to escape the commitment required for success. Even from the Cross Jesus fulfilled His responsibility to His family as we can read here in John.

> *26 When Jesus saw his mother standing there beside the disciple he loved, he said to her, "Dear woman, here is your son." 27 And he said to this disciple, "Here is your mother." And from then on this disciple took her into his home.* John 19:26-27 (NLT)

It is in this moment Jesus revealed that we must die to self and be responsible in the areas we are supposed to be. He could have focused on His unbearable pain, and ignored what He was supposed to do; He certainly would have been justified. He wasn't thinking about Himself, but was focused on meeting His responsibilities. He made sure His mother was taken care of before He died. His Kingdom is about others as we can read here in Philippians.

> *3 Don't be selfish; don't try to impress others. Be humble, thinking of others as better than yourselves. 4 Don't look out only for your own interests, but take an interest in others, too. 5 You must have the same attitude that Jesus had.* Philippians 2:3–5 (NLT)

This message applies to all of our relationships. If we are married, we have a responsibility to honor our vows in the covenant we have made, not just when our flesh feels like it. Women need to meet the needs of their husbands, and husbands need to meet the needs of their wives. If couples would choose to suffer and die to self in their marriage they would have an incredible fulfilling marriage!

I remember years ago reading the book "Men are from Mars and Women are from Venus." It talks about how men and women speak different languages and can't understand each other. I questioned God on that, asking Him why He would do that. His response was so we would die to self. Marriage was designed to kill our flesh. Marriages break up because our flesh refuses to die to selfishness. Marriage was not intended for us to kill each other, so we must stop trying to force our spouse to die! Instead we should choose to honor and prefer one another, to produce life in our marriage.

Often when I pray in my devotion time I cry out to God to help me die to myself, and transform me into the image of His Son. Then my husband gets up and says or does something (usually very innocently) that irritates me, and my flesh rises up and wants to react negatively. It is in that moment that I have a choice to "die to live or live to die." I will suffer by choice or by consequence. If I follow my flesh, there will be a price to pay, as an argument could follow, and then resentment will linger and keep us from peace and joy. During the time we allow strife in, the door is open for hell to come into our home. Alternatively by choice, I can change my hell into heaven by choosing to affirm and bless him, even when I don't feel like it. I can't tell you how many marriages would be saved if they simply obeyed this principle.

Recently while attending a Catholic funeral, the priest shared something that I thought was profound. He said that whenever he councils a newly engaged couple he puts a crucifix with Jesus on the Cross in front of the couple. He then asks if they think they are ready to get married. Usually the excited couple affirm positively that they indeed are. Then he turns to the soon-to-be groom, and asks him as he points to the crucifix, "Are you ready to do this for her?" He then repeats the question to the woman. He chuckled as he shared this usually results in shock and fear as the couples' replies are not as confident as when they first came to him. In some cases the engagement is called off. As interesting as this form of pre-marriage counseling is, it reveals the truth of the commitment we are making in Holy Matrimony. Are we ready to die to self to produce life in our marriages? I want to make a note here that dying to self does not mean enabling destructive behavior, but will confront in a spirit of love and humility when needed.

Our next responsibility is to our offspring. If you have children, you have responsibilities as a parent. Raising children requires a tremendous amount of sacrifice and dying to your flesh. Having children was also designed to humble us, challenge us, and stretch us beyond ourselves.

Children have a way of exposing who you really are, especially when you're trying to impress others. Shortly after I started pastoring, I remember having some members of our church over when my youngest daughter, who was supposed to be in bed, came prancing out into the living room with maxi pads stuck all over herself, announcing to us that she was the Easter bunny! As funny as it was, I was mortified as I was trying to make a good impression on our visitors. She is now thirty-two and may be mortified when I publish this story! (Parents can embarrass kids too.)

Another time one of my children humiliated me when I told a congregation member that I was busy the night before and couldn't get a job done that I was supposed to complete. My daughter, overhearing the conversation, piped up "No you weren't mommy, you were watching a movie!" Children will tell it like it is!

Our children are not impressed with our great accomplishments in life but with how much we care about them. It is easy to impress others, but our children know how we live. They see everything, and their beliefs are shaped by how we as parents live before them. Does our Christianity play out in our homes by loving and serving one another? Do we demonstrate God's Kingdom of love, peace, and joy? Do we practice gratitude and respect authority? Do we speak well of others? We have a responsibility to demonstrate the Spirit of Christ behind closed doors, as this will have great influence on our family when they choose who they will serve: God or the world.

We also have responsibilities at work, at church, in our community and country. Life is full of responsibility, and fulfilling our obligations requires suffering and dying to gain life.

Unfortunately our flesh wants to do what it wants to do regardless of the CONSEQUENCES to others. Many neglect church because they want to relax and enjoy a nice day, not realizing they are sending a message to their children that church isn't important. They aren't thinking about the vices that are in the world just waiting to get their grip on their children to destroy their lives. Church was designed to empower and connect people together to be strengthened and have a solid support system. The church also protects individuals from the many dangerous people in this world that try to take advantage of them and ultimately want to draw them away from God. Just as in the family, church is meant to cause us to grow in character and maturity by tests in our relationships with others. Running when we get offended is abandoning our responsibility and sending a message to our offspring that when the going gets tough, run!

Conflict happens in every relationship, but will it make or break us depending on how willing we are to suffer and die. The greater the sacrifices the greater and richer our relationships will become. I'm not advocating being used and abused, nor being a doormat. I'm referring to loving, honoring, and willingly serving those that you are responsible for, trusting God for His life to be produced in you.

Today, there is an epidemic of men and women walking away from their marriage vows. Many are abandoning their responsibilities as parents, ignoring the cries and needs of their broken-hearted children. Recently, I heard about a survey on the news asking young mothers if they were given

10,000 dollars would they spend it on themselves or invest it into the future of their children. The majority said they would spend it on themselves.

If we don't sacrifice for our children, we will suffer later. Consequences will come, and they will break our heart if we neglect our responsibility to them. It is better to choose our suffering by laying down our life for them now and trusting that they will be good, upright children of God who will bless us.

If we belong to a church, (and we should), we must choose to be responsible and contribute to the needs of our church. Whatever we commit to, we should be faithful to fulfill that commitment and do the best job we are able to. God loves the church; it is His body and it was His idea for us to meet in corporate gatherings. If everyone who connects to a local church does their share of volunteering and is faithful to give their tithes and offerings, the church would be able to function powerfully to impact their community: souls would be saved, marriages healed, and people's lives radically changed. Every need would be met. It is our responsibility to sow time and finances into our place of worship. Remember we are investing into the future of our children and grand-children and contributing to making a difference. Without the strong influence of the church our children would be easily influenced by the many things in the world that seek their destruction. It is our job to make the church strong. Too many Christians criticize and tear down their church and then wonder why their children don't want to serve God.

There is no perfect church; we can always find something to criticize, but instead choose to be thankful and be part of the solution not the problem. This is how you suffer now, but if you murmur and complain you will suffer later, and so will your children. You choose.

Another area of responsibility is in the workplace. In the world, most employers take advantage of their employees, and employees their employers. Dishonesty, laziness, and pleasure-seeking are now the norm. No wonder our prosperous nations are falling apart at the seams. Corruption is everywhere, threatening our peace and safety. Daily we hear about corruption in government, education systems, judicial systems, the workplace, and even some churches. Death is being sown because people aren't willing to die to self and produce the Kingdom of God, but instead are advancing hell.

Unfortunately, too many people are consumed with themselves. It's all about them, what they want or feel like doing. They have excuses for every selfish act and don't consider the consequences. Living in selfishness always produces death in the long run. We should not be deceived by temporary gratification at the expense of our responsibilities.

It is important if we want to change our hell into heaven that we list our God-given responsibilities. We must stop making excuses that keep us from fulfilling them and suffer and die where we are called to do so.

We are called to be responsible husbands or wives, parents, employees, or employers, and to be responsible at our church and in our community. Let's be a part of the solution not the problem, and we will find great peace and joy with contentment. There is nothing worth more than this because after we have suffered awhile by denying our flesh, we will experience heaven on earth. Our focus must be on the reward to come, and we will have the motivation to do what we are called to do.

Application to **CHANGE YOUR HELL INTO HEAVEN**

Read and meditate on Philippians 2:3–5

3 Don't be selfish; don't try to impress others. Be humble, thinking of others as better than yourselves. 4 Don't look out only for your own interests, but take an interest in others, too. 5 You must have the same attitude that Jesus had. Phil 2:3–5 (NLT)

STOP AND THINK about the seeds you are sowing in your family, church, job and other relationships. *You will reap what you sow. Evil deeds will have consequences when we give the devil and his demons access to hurt you and your loved ones. Your good seed will bring heaven on earth to you and your descendants.*

CHAPTER 6

IN THE THROES OF HELL

ne of the darkest moments on the Cross was when Jesus cried the most heart wrenching words, *"My God! My God! Why have you forsaken me!"* as we can read in Matthew 27:46 (NLT). When He bore all of our sin, the evil that enshrouded Him was overwhelming. Every horror that man has conceived was on Him, every murder, rape, lie, and immoral act. Greed, pride, hatred, fear and lust engulfed Him with their assault of pain, shame, and hopelessness. The pure and holy became the stench of filth and evil. Jesus was suffering and dying so life could be brought forth in us.

In life there are those horrific moments in time when the blackness of hell on earth seems to blind us from anything good. There are days when we think we can't go on another moment, and our will to live seems lost in a sea of pain and grief. Those are the days we call hell on earth.

I recall while watching a movie on the Holocaust feeling overwhelmed with grief over the aftermath of hundreds if not thousands of naked bodies thrown into mass graves. "How could this happen?" screamed in my mind! "How could God allow this?" "Where was He?" "Why?" "How?" When darkness is at its worst, Satan comes in like a flood bombarding us with fears and doubts, with judgments on God's response—or lack of it. I recently watched a movie called "Billy" about the early years of Billy Graham. It was told through the eyes of Charles Templeton, a close friend of Billy's who had fallen from his faith and denounced Christ. Charles was a great evangelist at one time; having crowds up to 30,000 people at his revival meetings. He helped Billy get started in his early years, working together with him to win souls. At the time World War II broke out, he was well known throughout the world as a great evangelist; but something happened. He began to judge and question God after witnessing the aftermath of the mass genocide that transpired in Europe under Hitler's reign of terror. His doubts overcame him, and after the death of his young daughter he could no longer believe in a God that would allow such things to happen. He positioned himself as God's judge.

Charles Templeton is not alone. Countless people have turned their backs on God when He didn't do what they thought He should and evil seemed to prevail. But there are others who rely on their faith, causing it to strengthen during the attacks that overwhelm them. I have discovered that we must know God through the Cross. *The work of the Cross is the physical manifestation of WHO GOD IS;* believing otherwise makes Him in our image and that is judging His character.

Jesus is the visible image of the invisible God. If you

have seen Him, you have seen the Father. Who are we to decide He is different than what the Cross says because of a circumstance we or someone we know may be going through? We must trust that God knows far more than our finite, limited thinking, and that His character is what the Cross demonstrated. If we trust in Him to be who He is, then we will trust that whatever happens will be what has to be for some reason or law that we don't yet understand. Our job is to trust in His character and obey Him.

It is our pride that struggles with this, and it is our pride that has to die. When we turn our backs on it and embrace Him, we will experience amazing life. That's what Billy Graham did when he was faced with the same challenge: when He was belittled and mocked by his best friend Charles Templeton for remaining steadfast in his faith.

Back in the seventies, shortly after I became a believer, I started attending a weekly meeting called "the Catacombs" held in downtown Toronto. It was there that I had the privilege of hearing an incredible man speak, Richard Wurmbrand. He had spent fourteen years in prison as a political prisoner and was tortured much of that time for His faith in Christ. He was arrested in 1948 when the Communists seized Romania and attempted to control the churches. Richard spent three of those years in solitary confinement where he preached sermons to himself to keep from going insane. For those years he did not see or talk to another human being apart from his Communist torturers, except for a fellow prisoner he communicated with by tapping Morris code on the cell wall. He was abandoned to rot in a dark dank cell.

Following his release he wrote a book containing many of those sermons called "Sermons in Solitary Confinement." One of them contained a pivotal message that forever lodged in my heart. He said, "No I will not deny Him. My mind does not know who He is or where He is. When I was strung up by my arms with my toes barely reaching the floor, and under similar tortures, I had no evidence that He exists. I was inclined to accuse Him as St. Theresa, the great Christian mystic, dared to accuse Him before me: 'O Lord, no wonder you have so few friends when you treat them so hard.' But I believe in the incomprehensible and terrible One. I believe that He is love, although at this moment I feel nothing of His love. I have to believe in its expression in a sacrifice two thousand years ago. I will not leave Him, nor deny Him, even if He leaves me." Wow, what powerful words of truth. Even though Richard was living in horrendous circumstances and had nothing in this world to give him any form of happiness, he found the true source of life within his spirit. He chose to worship and draw his strength from his faith in Christ's true character. Several years later he was released, and of prison he wrote, "The prison years did not seem too long for me, for I discovered, alone in my cell, that beyond belief and love there is delight in God : a deep and extraordinary ecstasy of happiness that is like nothing in this world." Incredible suffering has brought incredible life as God has used him to help countless other persecuted believers around the world through his ministry "The Voice of the Martyrs."

The big test will come for all of us. It comes in different ways and forms, but regardless of how; it leaves us reeling in fear, heartache, and hopelessness. It is the test of how real our faith and commitment to God really is. Let me clarify one thing, God does not test us, but life will. This world is under a curse, and sin abounds, giving birth to its devastating consequences. We hurt because of sin: ours and others'. Sin is sin because it steals, kills, and destroys God's most prized creation: us. When our flesh wants to blame and curse Him, will we keep our focus on the Cross and see God for who He really is? Will our hell kill us? Or will we be victorious and break through hell?

Losing a loved one is one of the most difficult, hellish experiences we can go through. As I shared in Chapter One, I remember clearly the crushing pain and grief I felt the day my husband Jim was killed in a car accident. Words cannot adequately describe the darkness and depth of anguish I felt. I could barely breathe, and the moments and days after seemed to drown me in so much pain that I didn't want to live anymore. I fought the most difficult battle of my life. I fought against anger, hatred, blame, hopelessness, and despair to name a few. I thought my life was over, and that pain and loneliness were never going to leave. In the midst of my hell I made a decision to love, to forgive, to serve, and to trust God no matter what. That choice wasn't easy. The enemy was still looming around me trying to knock me off course to make me give up, but when I made that decision, the cloud began to lift. Faith, joy, and peace began to return, and my desire to live was renewed. I chose to guard my heart and do what God's Word says regardless of how I felt. Remember God will deliver us from every trial if we trust Him as Psalm 34 tells us.

> *19 The righteous person faces many troubles, but the Lord comes to the rescue each time.*
> Ps 34:19 (NLT)

When we see the Cross as the eternal established statement of God's true character, we truly know Him. We can read about this is Colossians.

> *15 Christ is the visible image of the invisible God. He existed before anything was created and is supreme over all creation.* Col 1:15 (NLT)

If we see God through Christ, and Christ through the Cross, we will know His character of love, humility, unselfishness, mercy, and purity. It is then we are confident that nothing contradicting what it says about Him is true. Unfortunately, when our hell shows up, our flesh wants to lash out and accuse Him of the evil that is ripping us apart. We have a tendency to make God in our own image: who we decide He is. The Cross says God is love, merciful, humble, unselfish, faithful, just, giving, righteous, pure, and holy, to name a few of His key characteristics. But we sometimes accuse Him of being unjust, unloving, unkind, unfaithful, and evil. Some even curse Him and harden their hearts in their pride and anger refusing to trust Him anymore. This thinking creates a false god that leads us into deception and opens the door to hell in our life.

Suffering and dying to self is never easy. In fact, our natural man will fight it on every front. God requires that we leave nothing in us outside of His reign. Our hearts must be committed to Him in trust and gratitude even in our darkest, most horrific times. This kind of suffering and dying to self goes deep and often takes every ounce of faith and willpower we have. It reveals what is really in our hearts. However we are not alone, even though we may feel like it, because God is there watching and waiting for us to believe He is and that He rewards those who diligently seek Him. He will not leave or abandon us, but allow us to see the truth about the condition of our heart. How committed to Him are you? How well do you know His true character? Do you have faith that he has a better day for you?

Our darkest hour could be losing a child or having one on drugs. It could be an adulterous spouse, a ravaging disease, or loss of a job and in a mountain of debt. Whatever it is God remains the same. Gaze on the Cross and meditate on His character and refuse to believe the lies of hatred and blame. The Cross speaks hope, promise, life, and a future for us. We must lay down our fleshly cries to curse God and others and embrace the truth of the Cross. When we die to our flesh, life will come forth. When we embrace God and all His love for us, we can find joy and comfort even in our darkest hour.

Ephesians 3 says something so profound; we should

meditate on until we get it deep inside of us.

> *12 Because of Christ and our faith in him,*
> *we can now come boldly and confidently into*
> *God's presence. 13 So please don't lose heart*
> *because of my trials here. I am suffering for*
> *you, so you should feel honored. 14 When I*
> *think of all this, I fall to my knees and pray*
> *to the Father, 15 the Creator of everything*
> *in heaven and on earth. 16 I pray that from*
> *his glorious, unlimited resources he will*
> *empower you with inner strength through his*
> *Spirit. 17 Then Christ will make his home in*
> *your hearts as you trust in him. Your roots*
> *will grow down into God's love and keep you*
> *strong. 18 And may you have the power to*
> *understand, as all God's people should, how*
> *wide, how long, how high, and how deep his*
> *love is. 19 May you experience the love of*
> *Christ, though it is too great to understand*
> *fully. Then you will be made complete with all*
> *the fullness of life and power that comes from*
> *God. 20 Now all glory to God, who is able,*
> *through his mighty power at work within us,*
> *to accomplish infinitely more than we might*
> *ask or think.* Ephesians 3:12–20 (NLT)

The Apostle Paul was suffering great persecution because of his faith; however, his focus was not on his trials but on the incredible love of God that kept him grounded. Notice he says in verse 19 "may you experience the love of Christ," meaning knowledge that results from participating in that love. We must partake of that love, the full width, length, and depth of it, which will happen when we think about and meditate deeply on the work of the Cross. Whenever I choose to think about the suffering, death, and resurrection of Christ, I too, fall to my knees in overwhelming love and gratitude for all He has done for me. His humility, unselfishness, and total willingness to subject Himself to all the unbearable suffering motivated by His love for me blows me away. How could it not? It is then that we are made complete, whole, lacking nothing, and overflowing with His life and power! Wow! There is no greater joy, no closer place to heaven on earth! In fact I have discovered that the closest spot on earth to heaven is at the foot of the Cross. It is there that we see Him as He really is, and we see ourselves as we really are; sinners made righteous and immersed in His love when we least deserve it. What an awesome God!

Application to **CHANGE YOUR HELL INTO HEAVEN**

Read and meditate on Ephesians 3:12–20

12 Because of Christ and our faith in him, we can now come boldly and confidently into God's presence. 13 So please don't lose heart because of my trials here. I am suffering for you, so you should feel honored. 14 When I think of all this, I fall to my knees and pray to the Father, 15 the Creator of everything in heaven and on earth. 16 I pray that from his glorious, unlimited resources he will empower you with inner strength through his

Spirit. 17 Then Christ will make his home in your hearts as you trust in him. Your roots will grow down into God's love and keep you strong. 18 And may you have the power to understand, as all God's people should, how wide, how long, how high, and how deep his love is. 19 May you experience the love of Christ, though it is too great to understand fully. Then you will be made complete with all the fullness of life and power that comes from God. 20 Now all glory to God, who is able, through his mighty power at work within us, to accomplish infinitely more than we might ask or think. Ephesians 3:12 (NLT)

STOP AND THINK about the character of God. *Know God through the work of the Cross and refuse to believe lies about Him.* Don't allow anything to influence your judgment of His true character. Knowing Him for who He really is will give you security and faith in His promises.

** (Quoted from November 2011 Voice of the Martyr's Newsletter, p. 10.)

CHAPTER SEVEN

WHAT ARE YOU THIRSTING FOR?

O ur flesh is constantly bombarding us with what it wants. Feed me, pamper me, stop the pain, and give me what feels good when and how I want it! It never ceases to try to control every decision we make. We crave satisfaction and pleasure in one form or another to fill a void deep inside of us because cravings are the result of something lacking in our lives.

Sweets seem to call me relentlessly; they have a voice. My body craves the wrong foods and has an adverse desire for fresh fruits and vegetables. I eat when I'm stressed, happy, bored, sad, busy, or any other excuse that I can think of. I am surrounded by unhealthy food and opportunities to eat it; in fact, I think I would have to leave the planet to avoid this temptation completely. I do however have plenty of healthy choices as well. For me, junk food can be like a drug that satisfies the cravings I have for comfort. Unfortunately, there are consequences when I eat thoughtlessly. It is my flesh and emotions that want to take over and do what I know I shouldn't. Excess weight is only one of the side effects of an appetite out of control. Food ads should be labeled like a lot of prescription drugs are when advertised. They should say things like, "Eating this product can have adverse side effects such as high cholesterol, high blood pressure, weak knees and ankles, diabetes, heart attacks, bowel problems, stomach indigestion, apathy, lethargy, memory loss, insecurity, depression, and in some cases thoughts of suicide thoughts may occur." I'm sure you have seen the ads to sell prescription drugs. My husband and I have laughed at the long list of side effects wondering who would ever want to take them. To avoid all these consequences from food requires suffering and dying to the cravings in us. Giving into the voice of our flesh will produce hell in our lives and rob us of what we really desire: health, energy, and self-esteem, not to mention looking good!

Food is just one craving that we use to try to satisfy the needs and pain in our lives; some of us run to drugs, alcohol, sex, or gambling; some turn to other eating disorders or cutting. Some become workaholics or shopaholics. Whatever we use that is contrary to what is right and healthy for us will bring a negative consequence and will ultimately deepen our pain. We are not alone in this battle that wages inside of us. Jesus knew about our thirst as we can read here in John.

> *37 On the last day, the climax of the festival,*
> *Jesus stood and shouted to the crowds,*
> *"Anyone who is thirsty may come to me!*
> *38Anyone who believes in me may come and*

*drink! For the Scriptures declare, 'Rivers
of living water will flow from his heart."*
John 7:37–38 (NLT)

Here we can see that there is a solution to the unmet
needs we have. Jesus is the only one that can truly satisfy
our cravings. He is the answer to all that is wrong inside
of us. Yet in spite of this claim, He said something else in
the climax of His suffering, as we can read here in a later
passage in John.

*28 Jesus knew that his mission was now fin-
ished, and to fulfill Scripture he said, "I am
thirsty." John 19:28 (NLT)*

On the Cross Jesus uttered the cry *"I am thirsty!"* This
cry echoes from the heartfelt, gripping needs that destroy our
flesh and emotional well-being. It amazes me to know that
He, who is the only One who can really satisfy our thirst,
was Himself thirsting while on the Cross. The overwhelming
stench of our sin that was put on Him created the emptiness
and unfulfilled need in Him at that moment. He felt the thirst
that sin creates in us. The more we try to fill our deep needs
with the world's fulfillments, the greater the need becomes
inside of us. Sin will always produce more sin, more pain,
and more need. It's like a downward spiral into the deathly
grip of Satan himself, to trap and ensnare you; to keep you
powerless, unable to do or be who God has created you to
be. If we continue to satisfy the cravings of our flesh with the

things of this world, death will continue to be produced in us and our hell on earth will increase. If we choose to suffer and die to the bad habits that seek to destroy us, we will live.

Overcoming these ungodly cravings requires suffering by denying ourselves the pleasure of the moment. When we say "no" to unhealthy food, drugs, alcohol, immorality, or foolish spending, we choose to die to sin.

This powerful truth is found in 1 Peter 4.

> *1 So then, since Christ suffered physical pain, you must arm yourselves with the same attitude he had, and be ready to suffer, too. For if you have suffered physically for Christ, you have finished with sin. 2 You won't spend the rest of your lives chasing your own desires, but you will be anxious to do the will of God. 3 You have had enough in the past of the evil things that godless people enjoy—their immorality and lust, their feasting and drunkenness and wild parties, and their terrible worship of idols. 4 Of course, your former friends are surprised when you no longer plunge into the flood of wild and destructive things they do. So they slander you. 5 But remember that they will have to face God, who will judge everyone, both the living and the dead. 6 That is why the Good News was preached to those who are now dead—so although they were destined to die like all people, they now live forever with God in the Spirit. 1Peter 4:1 (NLT)*

Verse one tells us that when we are willing to suffer as Christ did, we have finished with sin! One day, we will all have to face God and give account for our actions. Do we want to spend the rest of our lives chasing deceptive desires that entrap and ruin us? Or do we want to do God's will and have abundant life? There is only one path to an overcoming life, and that is to suffer and die to our fleshly cravings. Only then will the amazing life of God fill us to overflowing with pure and holy gratitude and satisfaction. We can't have it both ways.

Because the cravings for the things of this world surround us relentlessly, we will always suffer when resisting them. "Buy me, eat me, enjoy this sexual experience, ease your pain with this drug" will show up all around us. Television, newspapers, stores ads, billboards, friends, and the Internet are some of the venues that entice your flesh with ways to satisfy your thirst by making false promises of happiness and satisfaction. There is a demonic realm of fallen angels behind these seducing voices desiring to rob us of the greatness and absolute joy, peace, and love we were created to have. They do everything to distract us from the source of living water.

We must die daily and keep our focus on the one who thirsted for us, and fills us with His healing and refreshing water. Drink of Him and you will be empowered to say "No!" in the times of temptation. Obviously, saying "no" to our fleshly desires can seem overwhelming and difficult at times. We can suffer intense withdrawal and even physical pain, but there is a wonderful promise in God's Word that will help you gain the victory in your moment of weakness.

This is a good scripture to memorize and quote when you need help resisting a temptation.

> *13 The temptations in your life are no dif-*
> *ferent from what others experience. And God*
> *is faithful. He will not allow the temptation*
> *to be more than you can stand. When you are*
> *tempted, he will show you a way out so that*
> *you can endure.* 1 Corinthians 10:13 (NLT)

WITH GOD THERE IS ALWAYS A WAY OUT. Remember that there is nothing you face that others haven't faced, also. As Christians we are temples of the Holy Spirit. That means that the very Spirit of God lives inside of us and gives us power and strength when we need it. We have been given the keys to overcome and conquer our flesh!

> *16 And I will ask the Father, and he will give*
> *you another Advocate, who will never leave*
> *you. 17 He is the Holy Spirit, who leads*
> *into all truth. The world cannot receive him,*
> *because it isn't looking for him and doesn't*
> *recognize him. But you know him, because he*
> *lives with you now and later will be in you.*
> John 14:16 (NLT)

In fact the Holy Spirit is the same Spirit that empowered Jesus to go through the Cross and rise from the dead and has now been released to live in us. We have unlimited strength and power available to us! But it doesn't work if we don't access Him and use the tools He has given us.

Just imagine you have been kidnapped by a serial killer

and he has bound you and locked you in a room somewhere. You are alone and overcome by fear, but every part of you kicks into survival mode as you desperately try to find a way out. Your desire to live is so strong that you are willing to try to escape, even at the risk of being caught and facing worse torture by angering your captor. You are trapped and can see no way out. Now imagine being in that situation with the Spirit of God, who knows exactly how you can escape, by simply asking for His help. Wouldn't you ask Him? We are all prey to Satan and his demons who find ways to deceive and keep us in sin. We are slaves to what controls us as it says here in 2 Peter.

2 Peter 2:19 19 *They promise freedom, but they themselves are slaves of sin and corruption. For you are a slave to whatever controls you.* John 14:19 (NLT)

The good news is we are not alone and we have been set free from slavery as we can read here in Galatians.

> *3 And that's the way it was with us before Christ came. We were like children; we were slaves to the basic spiritual principles of this world. 4 But when the right time came, God sent his Son, born of a woman, subject to the law. 5 God sent him to buy freedom for us who were slaves to the law, so that he could adopt us as his very own children. 6 And because we are his children, God has sent the Spirit of his Son into our hearts, prompting us to call out, "Abba, Father." 7 Now you are no longer a slave but God's own child. And since you are his child, God has made you*

74

*his heir. 8 Before you Gentiles knew God,
you were slaves to so-called gods that do not
even exist. 9 So now that you know God (or
should I say, now that God knows you), why
do you want to go back again and become
slaves once more to the weak and useless
spiritual principles of this world?* Galatians
4:3–9 (NLT)

We have been called out of slavery to sonship in God.
He has given us His Spirit to empower us to break free of
the bondage of sin and destroy the works of darkness from
over us. Our sin is what destroys us and keeps us from our
inheritance from God. We are heirs of God's Kingdom and
all it offers us. It is incredible and powerfully liberating
when we truly understand this.

Why not ask the Holy Spirit to show you the way out
of your temptation, along with the strength to take it? He
promises us a way of escape and is waiting for you to call
on Him.

***Our responsibility is to thirst for Him, not something
else.*** When we turn to Him to satisfy our needs, and heal our
wounds we will find eternal overflowing life. Remember
when Jesus cried *"I thirst,"* he was declaring what sin does
to us. Quit drinking from the cup of contaminated, filthy,
scummy water that leaves you sick, discouraged, and broken
and choose to drink from the pure, holy, refreshing water
that He offers; it will change your hell into heaven.

Application to **CHANGE YOUR HELL INTO HEAVEN**

Read and meditate on 2 Peter 2:19 and 1 Corinthians 10:13

> *19 They promise freedom, but they them-selves are slaves of sin and corruption. For you are a slave to whatever controls you.* 2 Peter 2:19 (NLT)

> *13 The temptations in your life are no dif-ferent from what others experience. And God is faithful. He will not allow the temptation to be more than you can stand. When you are tempted, he will show you a way out so that you can endure.* 1 Corinthians 10:13 (NLT)

STOP AND THINK when you are faced with a choice to do what is right or wrong, that *you are not alone in your temptation. God has promised a way out. Ask Him to show you the way and you will find it.* Resisting temptation will close the door to hell in your life.

CHAPTER EIGHT

WHAT ARE YOU
FINISHED WITH?

I remember March 1971, the month that I gave my life to Jesus Christ. I was changed instantly by a prayer. I was finished with immoral living, drugs, alcohol and swearing. It took me a few years however to be finished with smoking though I had made many attempts. It wasn't until my young daughter informed me that when I smoked I was burning Jesus in my heart. Of course I knew that wasn't true, but I was convicted! Shortly afterwards I had my last cigarette.

We are each on our own journey with Christ. When He cried, "It is finished!" from the Cross, He had done all that was needed for us to walk a victorious Christian life. The journey we are on in life has a definite destination and purpose. 1 Peter tells us that we are temporary residents here, chosen for a higher purpose, and we are called to finish that purpose.

> *9 But you are not like that, for you are a chosen people. You are royal priests, a holy nation, God's very own possession. As a result,*

you can show others the goodness of God, for he called you out of the darkness into his wonderful light. 10 "Once you had no identity as a people; now you are God's people. Once you received no mercy; now you have received God's mercy." Dear friends, I warn you as "temporary residents and foreigners" to keep away from worldly desires that wage war against your very souls. 1 Peter 2:9–12 (NLT)

Notice that it says we are foreigners here, temporary residents. If Christ doesn't return first we have a one hundred percent chance of dying. We are passing through, on our way to an eternity with God, who desires that we keep our focus on the life to come. We can read about this in Colossians.

Since you have been raised to new life with Christ, set your sights on the realities of heaven, where Christ sits in the place of honor at God's right hand. 2 Think about the things of heaven, not the things of earth. 3 For you died to this life, and your real life is hidden with Christ in God. 4. And when Christ, who is your life, is revealed to the whole world, you will share in all his glory. Col 3:1–4 (NLT)

We are to set our sights on the realities of heaven. Over history there are many people that have gone on pilgrimages for spiritual reasons. I have gone to Israel numerous times to experience and see the places in the Bible and grow in my understanding of the Scriptures. To achieve success on a pilgrimage, we must leave our comforts of home and bring only what is necessary to survive the possible hardships of the trip. We also need to keep our focus on completing the journey and be willing to endure whatever it takes to reach our desired goals.

Professional athletes know the time and sacrifices that they have to make to excel in their field. There is usually great sacrifice and suffering involved in attaining anything that is of great value! However when your focus is on the desired goal, the journey, though difficult, becomes easier.

As we go through life we make decisions concerning what we will or will not do. As Christians we live by standards as we establish what we feel is right or wrong for us. Some Christians refuse to watch any form of TV or go to a movie theater. Some allow only family friendly programs or shows to entertain them, while others will watch almost anything. All Christians have different convictions for the many areas of their lives.

We are continually deciding what we should or should not do. God's Holy Spirit lives inside of us and deep down in our hearts, He gives us guidance for these choices. The Word is very clear on sexually moral issues, idolatry, greed, hatred, selfishness, lying, cheating, stealing etc. We simply need to read the Ten Commandments to find the basic laws of right and wrong, however there are many grey areas that can vary from person to person. Drinking is one of them.

Some Christians have never tasted alcohol. They have strong conviction to totally abstain. I know others that have an occasional glass of wine and feel at complete peace about their choice. We are not to judge the motives or hearts of fellow believers on issues not clearly condemned in God's Word. Obviously getting drunk is condemned, however a little wine is actually encouraged in scripture.

Because I am a leader I never want to be a stumbling block to someone with a drinking problem, therefore I have made my choice. I am perfectly happy and content not drinking and have no desire to, but that is a personal conviction I have. I do not wish to impose my convictions on someone else, as that is not my job. Nor should I think I'm better than or judge someone that chooses to drink. Our job is to be obedient to God and do what He tells us to do individually.

The Bible tells us we need to be led by the Spirit of God in all we do. This is how Jesus lived His life. The Spirit is in us for the purpose of helping us in all we do. We simply have to acknowledge Him and ask for His help. Jesus said He would always be with us, and when we follow Him we will find life as we can read here in Romans.

1 So now there is no condemnation for those who belong to Christ Jesus. 2 And because you belong to him, the power of the life-giving Spirit has freed you from the power of sin that leads to death. 3 The law of Moses was unable to save us because of the weakness of our sinful nature. So God did what the law could not do. He sent his own Son in a body like the bodies we sinners have. And in that body God declared an end to sin's control over us by giving his Son as a sacrifice for our sins. 4 He did this so that the just requirement of the law would be fully satisfied for us, who no longer follow our sinful nature but instead follow the Spirit. Romans 8:1–4 (NLT)

We are all so uniquely made and are from different cultures and family backgrounds, and only the Holy Spirit knows what we can or cannot handle.. He will lead and warn us about anything that would be a threat to our well-being. We are called to work out our own salvation as we read here in Philippians 2.

12 Wherefore, my beloved, as ye have always obeyed, not as in my presence only, but now much more in my absence, work out your own salvation with fear and trembling. Philippians 2:12 (NLT)

Once I know the will of God for me, I have a responsibility to walk out what He tells me. I need to be finished with disobedience because that is the major sin we each contend with. God is much more concerned about the sins of the heart, and WHY we do things. He is looking for those who have a heart after Him, hear His voice and DO WHAT HE SAYS!

We need to be finished with our self-will and ungrateful, rebellious and prideful nature! On the Cross Jesus cried out the words, "It is finished," and those words meant a multitude of things that He paid for and finished! Finished is the condemnation of the law, finished is our separation from God; finished is our powerlessness and slavery to sin! We are redeemed from the curse, Satan is under our feet, and we have access to the very throne of God. We have been made righteous and transformed from sinners to saints. The following scriptures from 1 John validate this.

> *5 And you know that Jesus came to take away our sins, and there is no sin in him. 6 Anyone who continues to live in him will not sin.* **But anyone who keeps on sinning does not know him or understand who he is.** *7 Dear children, don't let anyone deceive you about this: When people do what is right, it shows that they are righteous, even as Christ is righteous. 8 But when people keep on sinning, it shows that they belong to the devil, who has been sinning since the beginning. But the Son of God came to destroy the works of the devil.* 1 John 3:5–9 (NLT)

Hebrews tells us that God is always available to us when we need His help and His grace empowers us to do His will.

> *But if we pursue sin, then we do not really know Him; however, when we desire to overcome sin He will give us grace, His divine enablement, when we need help. So let us come boldly to the throne of our gracious God. There we will receive his mercy, and we will find grace to help us when we need it most.* Hebrews 4:16 (NLT)

Jesus finished the entire will of God for His life, not leaving one thing out. When we doubt Him, we sin by trusting in ourselves more than His promises. We do not even come close to doing what He did. We did not destroy the works of the devil; He did. He opened the door to freedom for us all!

He has made the way for us to be finished with the things of this world, and say NO to what draws us away from God, so His glory will be in us when we finish well.

> *12 Dear friends, don't be surprised at the fiery trials you are going through, as if something strange were happening to you. 13 Instead, be very glad—for these trials make you partners with Christ in his suffering, so that you will have the wonderful joy of seeing his glory when it is revealed to all the world. 14 So be happy when you are insulted for being a Christian, for then the glorious Spirit of God rests upon.* 1 Peter 4: 12 (NLT)
> *15 Do not love this world nor the things it offers you, for when you love the world, you do not have the love of the Father in you. 16 For the world offers only a craving for physical pleasure, a craving for everything we see, and pride in our achievements and possessions. These are not from the Father, but are from this world.* 1 John 2:15—16 (NLT)

God is more glorious and awesome than anything this world has to offer! We settle for so much less than what He has for us; therefore, we must be finished with our limited thinking. We must see ourselves as children of God who are recipients of all His promises when we meet the conditions He has for us.

When we pursue God and focus on what He has done for us, we will be so consumed with Him that we will hate sin as He does. We will see it for what it really is, misleading and destructive. We will also love the sinner more and grieve for them to know God as we do. That is why God commands that we love Him with our whole heart, mind, soul, and strength. It is then that our whole being comes into alignment with God, and we become like Him as we were created to be. We were originally made in His image, and the whole purpose of our redemption and reconciliation with Him is to bring us back to the image we were made in. This process opposes our fallen nature and the desires of our flesh. The good news is that as we feed our spirit with God's Word, and focus on His Cross and His promises, our spirit grows stronger and our flesh becomes weaker. If we spend hours focusing on the things this world offers we feed our flesh, and we remain captive to its desires. We must make the decision to be finished with feeding our flesh, and choose to feed our spirit.

Rick and I recently did a minor landscaping job in front of our home. Neither of us is gifted with a green thumb, but to save money we decided to do it ourselves. We discovered that if we ever had to live off the land we would probably starve! Kidding aside, we did learn something. After using weed killer on the weeds, we planted five shrubs and a small tree. Once they were all in the ground we laid down some cloth designed to prevent the weeds from growing. We made sure that the new plants had plenty of rich soil around them and watered them with water that had been enriched with plant food to help them grow. We were doing everything we could to ensure that they would survive and the weeds would not. That's what we need to do with our spirit.

God has given us tools to feed our spirit. We have all we need to grow. His Spirit is in us to guide us; we have His Word and authority over the devil. We also have access to His throne through prayer and great and precious promises. He has also given us apostles, prophets, evangelists, pastors, and teachers, to equip us for the work we are called to do.

Let's be honest before God and ask His Spirit to empower us to be finished with anything that brings death into our lives. As we learn His Word, and pray, immersing ourselves in sound teaching and good fellowship, we will overflow with His grace and power. This will cause us to grow and mature in every good work!

It is not how you start the race that matters, but how you finish. To be finished with our old sinful nature and the world's systems will cause some suffering as we make these hard choices, but the results will be liberating. To be finished with our cravings for physical pleasure, craving for all we see, and for the accolades of this world, requires suffering. Be determined to finish the course God has called you to.

What is the Holy Spirit telling you to be finished with? What is He telling you to do? Obey Him even when it causes you suffering and see the joy of your salvation burst forth with life more abundantly.

He has promised us His life; He will change your hell into heaven.

Application to **CHANGE YOUR HELL INTO HEAVEN**

Read and meditate on 1 John 2:15 and 1 Peter 4:12–14

> *Do not love this world nor the things it offers you, for when you love the world, you do not have the love of the Father in you. 16 For the world offers only a craving for physical pleasure, a craving for everything we see, and pride in our achievements and possessions. These are not from the Father, but are from this world. 1John 2:15 (NLT)*

> *Dear friends, don't be surprised at the fiery trials you are going through, as if something strange were happening to you. 13 Instead, be very glad—for these trials make you partners with Christ in his suffering, so that you will have the wonderful joy of seeing his glory when it is revealed to all the world. 14 So be happy when you are insulted for being a Christian, for then the glorious Spirit of God rests upon. 1 Peter 4: 12 (NLT)*

STOP AND THINK about *the things in your life that you should be finished with, and use the tools that He has given you to conquer them and finish well.* On the Cross He destroyed the power of sin from over you and made provision for you to be victorious over anything that would try to destroy you.

CHAPTER NINE

YOU ARE NOT YOUR OWN!

The last words uttered from the lips of Jesus, can be found in Luke 23:46 Then Jesus shouted, "Father, I entrust my spirit into your hands!" And with those words he breathed his last. These are the ultimate words of faith. God had just put Him through the hell of hells yet He still trusted Him.

Trusting God is not easy at first and there have been many times I have stepped out in faith with fear and trembling. One such time occurred shortly after my husband Rick and I were married. It began when the only means of transportation for a large family in our church, a beat up old conversion van, kept breaking down on them. They did not have the finances to replace it, so I began praying that God would provide for them. Almost instantly the Lord instructed me to give them our two year old van.

When I told Rick, he was not at all open to do this, as we didn't have the money to purchase another vehicle. At that time we had our six teenagers living with us and only one other car that they shared. Feeling very convicted that I had heard from God I coaxed Rick to pray about it, which he reluctantly agreed to do. Shortly after he began praying about it, we started having serious problems with both vehicles. Every day one or the other had to go for repairs due to mechanical problems, flat tires, or some form of malfunction. Finally, after thirty days of this, Rick was driving downtown in our city, when flames started shooting out of the steering wheel of the van. He had to pull over quickly to a nearby service station and use their fire extinguisher to douse the flames. He came home that day resigned to the fact that he now believed we were to give it away. We repaired everything and then called the family to let them know that we were giving them our vehicle in obedience to God. They were overjoyed.

Rick however made me promise not to pressure him to buy another car, we would either go without, or God would have to provide. In my spirit I knew God was going to do something, but I felt very nervous about it. If He didn't, Rick was not going to be thrilled about having to use the beat-up old car that belonged to our kids. Several days went by, and nothing seemed to happen. My fear began to grow that we would be stuck without adequate transportation. After five days without our van, I went into the sanctuary of our church to pray, begging God for any vehicle to help meet our needs. I had started out believing for a specific one, but now I was getting desperate! My faith was being tested, and I was experiencing a bit of fear and trembling.

It was a Wednesday afternoon, and while I was praying I heard God's voice say that my answer was here. I rushed from the sanctuary into the office area and saw no one. Our receptionist however said someone had called and needed to see us for a few minutes. I knew inside of me that it had something to do with God's provision, so I told Rick we needed to make this call. We phoned this individual, who immediately came by and nervously sat down in Rick's office. He was a fairly new believer in our church, and he started the conversation by telling us that he didn't really understand what was going on, but he had been unable to sleep for several days because he felt he was supposed to buy us a new vehicle. He was there to tell us that he and a co-worker would buy us a brand new car of our choice and asked what we wanted. We had been praying for a particular van, and by the end of that day we left a car lot with the answer to our prayers! God is faithful! What a testimony this was to our children, who all thought we were crazy for giving away our van. Not only did our faith grow, but theirs did too.

Even though fear is the opposite of faith, you conquer it by not allowing it to dictate your choices. Even though I may still FEEL fear, my actions determine the outcome.

Absolute surrender and trust is your greatest victory but it requires suffering and dying to self in order to gain victory. *Surrendering means you have more faith in God than you do in yourself.* Faith in God demands humility. The more pride we operate in, the more we are activating Satan's realm giving him power in our lives. The more we humble ourselves in abandonment and trust, the more we activate God's power in our lives.

To be able to totally trust God and rely on His ability to finish the work He started in us is difficult for most of us. As I said earlier, there is something about us that desires to do what we want, when we want and how we want. In fact, judging by our actions we really believe that we know what is best for us more than God does. (pride) When we really think this through, it is very amusing to actually believe we know better than Him! To suffer and die to our own personal self-exaltation is a challenge and stirs up fears that intimidate us.

As humans, our greatest abilities consist of what we know and have experienced in our little world, which is so small compared to the vast amount of what exists in creation. It is true that we have amazing brains and are quite capable of brilliant things, but for the most part, regardless of how intelligent we are or how much we know, we are extremely limited in gifts, talents, and knowledge compared to God, who is all-powerful and all-knowing and omnipresent. Even the most brilliant brain surgeon may not know how a computer works or be able to fix a car or write a song. Most people are very gifted and knowledgeable in something, maybe a few things, but not much more. That's why we need each other and most of all why we all need God.

I know that I have the gift to teach, get good ideas, and motivate vision, but the details to get things done stress me out! Therefore I try to surround myself with people that are good at doing what I'm weak in. We are all part of something so much greater than ourselves, connected and dependent on others. I need a personal assistant, receptionist, co-leaders, hairdresser, doctor, dentist and even experts in technology, to name a few. To work with people does require trust. People can disappoint us, and betray us occasionally, but more than all the people I depend on, I need God. He created and understands every part of me. He knows the beginning from the end, the decisions I will make, and the motives of my heart, along with everyone else's. He created every resource on this planet and holds everything together—and gifted us with the ability to create from what He provides. He made every star, planet, and moon. Everything was created for Him, and nothing exists without Him as we can read here in John.

> *1 In the beginning the Word already existed. The Word was with God, and the Word was God. 2 He existed in the beginning with God. 3 God created everything through him, and nothing was created except through him. 4 The Word gave life to everything that was created, and his life brought light to everyone. 5 The light shines in the darkness, and the darkness can never extinguish it.* John 1:1 (NLT)

If we really believe this scripture, we should have great respect and trust that God may know a lot more about what is best for us than we do. Perhaps we do believe God is the creator of all things, and knows everything, but our issue is more about TRUSTING Him.

WE TRUST GOD TO THE DEGREE WE REALLY KNOW HIM.

To abandon and surrender yourself to someone or something requires total trust and faith in whom or what you are surrendering to. This is why it is so important to really know God through His actions and words. Trust comes with relationship.

The work of the Cross is the ultimate demonstration of God's character and proof of the truth of what His Word says about Him and that He can be trusted. Just think about what He did. I cannot possibly see God through the Cross and think He can't be trusted nor believe that He doesn't have my best interest in His heart. Doubt and unbelief are a big problem in us. When we have more faith in ourselves and our abilities than God's, we minimize Him and exalt ourselves.

Whenever we think or act like we know more than God, we are trusting in ourselves over Him. This is the ultimate sin and will keep us from heaven on earth in our circumstances. In fact, it partners with the forces of hell, opposing God as Lucifer did when he fell from heaven. Let's read what the scripture says about this.

> *12 How art thou fallen from heaven, O Lucifer, son of the morning! how art thou cut down to the ground, which didst weaken the nations! 13 For thou hast said in thine heart, I will ascend into heaven, I will exalt my throne above the stars of God: I will sit also upon the mount of the congregation, in the sides of the north: 14 I will ascend above*

the heights of the clouds; I will be like the most High. Isaiah 14:12 KJV

Notice in Verse 13 it says that he (Satan) wanted to exalt his throne above the stars of God, and be like God in verse 14. He wanted to be God. This is the ultimate spirit of pride, and it took him down. Anytime we exalt ourselves over God, we are setting ourselves up for a fall. Throughout the Word of God we read numerous accounts of God holding back His blessings because of this sin as He did here with Moses and Aaron.

> *12 But the Lord said to Moses and Aaron, "Because you did not trust me enough to demonstrate my holiness to the people of Israel, you will not lead them into the land I am giving them!"* Numbers 20:12 (NLT)

Lack of trust kept Moses and Aaron from the Promised Land, and it can keep you from it too.

We can read here in Psalms that we need to search for God to truly know and trust Him, and when we do we will be assured and secure in Him.

> *10 Those who know your name trust in you, for you, O Lord, do not abandon those who search for you.* Psalms 9:10 (NLT)

To know God is to trust Him!

In Proverbs we can read how we must not depend on our limited knowledge and understanding, but we are to trust

93

Him with ALL of our heart, not just a small portion of it. Every part of our lives belongs to Him and we must trust that He will orchestrate every compartment of our being to bring us life and fulfillment.

> *5 Trust in the Lord with all your heart; do not depend on your own understanding.* Proverbs 3:5 (NLT)

> *20 Those who listen to instruction will prosper; those who trust the Lord will be joyful.* Proverbs 16:20 (NLT)

Isaiah talks about how we can stay in perfect peace when we choose to trust Him, and ***FIX our thoughts on Him***. Fixing our thoughts means we don't waver or stray from thinking His thoughts, but we constantly meditate on His Word and remember what He did for us at the Cross.

> *3 You will keep in perfect peace all who trust in you, all whose thoughts are fixed on you!* Isaiah 26:3 (NLT)

We can choose what we think about, and God should dominate our thoughts. That doesn't mean that we never think of anything else, but that His influence embraces whatever we do think about.

The opposite of trusting Him is unbelief or faithlessness, which is the ultimate rejection of who He is. Jesus often addressed that issue as we can read in the following.

17 Jesus said, "You faithless and corrupt people! How long must I be with you? How long must I put up with you? Bring the boy here to me." Matthew 17:17 (NLT)

When we have no faith, we are powerless to walk in victory, and remain stuck in the circumstances that destroy us because we are putting faith in our abilities instead of His. When we are in doubt and unbelief God's power is limited in our lives, but as it says here in Hebrews we please Him when we have faith in Him

6 And it is impossible to please God without faith. Anyone who wants to come to him must believe that God exists and that he rewards those who sincerely seek him. Hebrews 11:6 (NLT)

To have faith in God is not a trivial thing, it is most important! Everything He does is activated by faith. It is the power switch to the supernatural and entrance to His Kingdom. The Bible says that the just shall live by faith, and faith comes by hearing the Word of God.[***]

Jesus trusted the Father up to His dying breath, and He suffered for it and He died for it, but then He defeated death and rose again because of it! That is the way God wants us to live in every circumstance in life.

Do you trust the Father with every part of your being? Do you trust Him enough to suffer for Him? Or do you trust yourself? Will you die to yourself to find life, or live for yourself and forfeit the eternal promises God offers?

You can change your hell into heaven by suffering and dying to self, and allowing His life to intervene in your circumstances. It's the only way.

Application to **CHANGE YOUR HELL INTO HEAVEN**

Read and meditate on Hebrews 11:6 and Proverbs 3:5

> *6 And it is impossible to please God without faith. Anyone who wants to come to him must believe that God exists and that he rewards those who sincerely seek him.* Hebrews 11:6 (NLT)

> *5 Trust in the L lord with all your heart; do not depend on your own understanding.* Proverbs 3:5 (NLT)

STOP AND THINK about *WHO you are REALLY PUTTING YOUR TRUST IN, God or yourself? Choose to trust Him, **LET GO AND LET GOD!*** Remember that He knows you better than yourself, and He is more than able and willing to take care of everything you surrender to Him. Start surrendering those things that you have been trying to take care of yourself.

***Taken from Romans 10:17

CHAPTER TEN

MAKE IT YOUR FINAL DECISION

We are all called by God to suffer and die in order to produce life. The scriptures reveal this is the only way to change our hell into heaven. Going through the suffering makes it worth it if you are fixed on the rewards to be gained. The key is; are we looking at the suffering or the reward to come?

This is the surest way to produce true life as we can read here in John 12.

> *24 I tell you the truth, unless a kernel of wheat is planted in the soil and dies, it remains alone. But its death will produce many new kernels—a plentiful harvest of new lives. 25 Those who love their life in this world will lose it. Those who care nothing for their life in this world will keep it for eternity. 26 Anyone who wants to be my disciple must follow me, because my servants must be where I am. And the Father will honor anyone who serves me. John 12: 24–26 (NLT)*

There are multitudes of people who do not know God but are willing to suffer to get what they really want. They endure suffering by keeping their eyes on their goal. Exercise is a great example of this. I know many nonbelievers that sweat it out, causing aches and pains to their bodies, in order to be healthier and leaner. The *Biggest Loser* TV show is an example of how much people are willing to endure to reach their goal. I have seen people torture themselves just to lose weight. Others will sacrifice by saving and not spending money on things they would love to have, being willing to go without for the sake of staying out of debt and being financially free. Every woman who has ever had a baby was willing to go through some suffering and was willing to die to her pride in order to give birth to a new life. Even after experiencing the horrific pain of childbirth, most are willing to do it again. Everything from sports, education, business, and entertainment require suffering by commitment, hard work, and sacrifice to come out on top. There are no short-cuts in life. These are just a few examples of dying to the flesh for a better reward. Suffering is not a new concept. To get what we really want demands it.

The last words of Jesus reveal the key areas we are called to die to self and live unto God. We will overcome our temptation if we obey the Spirit in these important responsibilities. It is much easier when we Embrace suffering as part of the process to obtain the true blessings we desire.

One other key we need to apply in this process is our attitude. Suffering with the right attitude makes a huge difference in the results that we will have, and make the process much more enjoyable! We can suffer with joy and peace or self-pity and complaints.

We can see good or bad in anything. Many people who seem to have everything are miserable. They live in discontent and never see the blessings in their life. Others have very little but are overflowing with contentment and joy. It's how we choose to see it. *A good attitude will get us everywhere.* It will open doors for us and draw people to us. We may not always be able to choose our circumstance but we can always choose our attitude.

Years ago, before we gave our van away, I was praying for a woman with a large family. (I have to be careful who I pray for!) God told me to give her my washing machine. I had just purchased it, and it was the first one I had owned. After years of having to bring all of my laundry to a laundromat, it meant a lot to me and I loved that machine. For days I argued with God, trying to get out of His request, until I couldn't even pray anymore without feeling convicted about it. Finally, I gave in and reluctantly called the woman He had told me to bless with it. When she asked if I was sure I wanted to give it to her, I responded curtly with "Yes, I am!" I was not happy about it and definitely had a wrong attitude, but was being obedient in spite of how I felt. I definitely wasn't giving it with joy. When she and her husband came by to pick it up, they discovered that they would need to install the proper hook up for it in their basement before taking it. They told me they would come back for it, but they didn't return for it for a year.

In the meantime, I began learning about the blessings of giving. The more I learned, the more excited I became and looked for opportunities to give. By the time this couple returned for the washing machine, I was thrilled to bless them with it. The day they picked it up, I had to leave my home at the same time they did, and followed their truck thanking and praising God for the privilege I had in blessing them. I was overcome with joy, even though I now had nothing to wash my clothes with. While I was praising God, I heard Him say that He was going to bless me. The following day, I received an unexpected large cheque in the mail from some insurance company that I knew nothing about. They apparently owed it to me from several years before, and the amount enabled me to buy a new machine with money left over!

I thank God that He dealt with my attitude before I parted with my washer, or I would have missed the reward. God is not just looking for obedience but for *how* we obey. This was one of many times God has spoken to me about giving, which has become a way of life for me. Whenever we give our tithes and offerings, we need to do an attitude check. Some may give begrudgingly and miss the reward that comes with giving with a grateful heart.

God reveals in His Word that we should have great joy in suffering. He didn't simply say to have joy, but to have GREAT joy. That means we should overflow with it. When we understand this, we will be excited about the trials that we go through. Why? It's not because of the suffering, but the reward that is to follow. We can read this in James.

Dear brothers and sisters, when troubles come your way, consider it an opportunity for great joy. 3 For you know that when your faith is tested, your endurance has a chance to grow. 4 So let it grow, for when your endurance is fully developed, you will be perfect and complete, needing nothing. James 1:2–4 (NLT)

Suffering is an opportunity for something greater! It births life, gives us reward, empowers us and leaves us needing nothing! What can be better than that? Just hours before Jesus chose to embrace His passion He revealed His heart and the attitude which motivated Him as He suffered and died. It is found in 1 Corinthians.

23 For I pass on to you what I received from the Lord himself. On the night when he was betrayed, the Lord Jesus took some bread, 24 and gave thanks to God for it. Then he broke it in pieces and said, "This is my body, which is given for you. Do this to remember me." 1 Corinthians 11:23–24 (NLT)

I want you to notice that on the night He was BETRAYED, He took the bread and gave THANKS. He didn't just thank God when all was going well for Himself, but He thanked Him when He knew He had been betrayed and was about to go through His greatest nightmare. Thanking God when we are hurting is not easy if we focus on the pain. Our flesh wants to complain and cry out in self-pity. It loves the negative attention and the expression of how bad things are so others will cater to it. But not Jesus; He chose His suffering with dignity and thanksgiving and purposely walked through hell, experiencing all of its torment, hopelessness, and pain, to come out on the other side as the greatest champion ever. He led the way into an eternity in heaven not for Himself, but for you and I. As we embrace Him in every area of our lives, transformation will come, and we will be conformed to His image as we were created to be.

We can do this with an attitude of gratitude, by focusing on the complete redemptive work of the Cross: the suffering, death, and resurrection. Let thanksgiving for what He has already done for you motivate your heart as you die to self and focus on eternity and the rewards God promises us.

In summary, our dying Saviour reveals what we are called to do to change our hell into heaven.

1. **STOP AND THINK** about the suffering Jesus went through for us that led to His resurrection. *The key to changing our hell into heaven is to know that we must choose to suffer and die to self to gain the life on the other side of our suffering.*

2. **STOP AND THINK** that whatever we choose to do will be a witness (good or bad) to the people we influence; therefore *choose the path of humility by obedience to God. This will position us to be richly blessed by God and experience heaven on earth!*

3. **STOP AND THINK** of how much we have been forgiven;

which will change our perspective and give us apprecia-tion for God who empowers us to forgive. This breaks the chains of bondage from our lives and frees us from a life of hell in the gall of bitterness and unforgiveness.

4. **STOP AND THINK** *of the many hurting and lost people who need hope, and focus on their need rather than our own, fulfilling our God-given responsibilities.*

5. **STOP AND THINK** about the responsibilities and the seeds you are sowing by your choices. *You will reap what you sow as no evil deed will go without consequence. Doing evil hurts you and gives demons access to your loved ones. Your good seed will bring heaven on earth to you and your descendants.*

6. **STOP AND THINK** about the character of God. *Know Him through the work of the Cross and refuse to believe lies about Him. Your circumstances will try to convince you that He is unjust, unloving, and unrighteous.* Don't allow anything to influence your judgment concerning His true character that was proven through the redemptive work of the Cross. Knowing Him for who He really is will give you security and faith in His promises.

7. **STOP AND THINK** when you are faced with temptation that *you are not alone and God has promised a way out. Ask Him to show you the way, and you will find it.* Resisting temptation will close the door to hell in your life.

8. **STOP AND THINK** about *the things in your life that you should be finished with, and use the tools that He has given you to conquer them and finish well.* On the Cross

He destroyed the power of sin from over you and made provision for you to be victorious over anything that would try to destroy you.

9. **STOP AND THINK** about *WHOM you are trusting; God or yourself. Choose to trust in Him and His love for you, knowing that He knows you better than yourself and will do only what is best for you.*

10. **STOP AND THINK** *about your attitude: are you grateful or discontent? Choose to be thankful by remembering all that God has already done for you and keep your thoughts on His goodness.* We can choose to focus on our blessings or on our problems. One brings heaven and the other hell. You choose.

Remember suffering will come because we live in a world full of sin, death and hell. He is the Light and has brought Hope for all to see the way to life. Choose to walk in the light, to be like Him. Then and only then will you be overflowing with righteousness, peace, and joy, walking and establishing the Kingdom of God as His true children. Listen to these powerful words of Jesus in John and let them permeate deep into your heart.

> *35 Jesus replied, "My light will shine for you just a little longer. Walk in the light while you can, so the darkness will not overtake you. Those who walk in the darkness cannot see where they are going. 36 Put your trust in the light while there is still time; then you will*

become children of the light." John 12: 35
(NLT)

There is great joy for those who walk in the light, the darkness cannot overtake them. That means when heaven comes, hell must go. His light will drive out the darkness.

Choose your suffering, don't be a victim of it. As I said before when you choose to deny your flesh and suffer for Christ you will live, but when you choose to satisfy the lusts of your flesh you will reap untold suffering and bring hell and death into your life.

STOP AND THINK ABOUT IT.
YOU HAVE THE POWER TO CHANGE YOUR HELL INTO HEAVEN!

About the Author

~

Cathy is an inspiring teacher and leader who travels and speaks internationally with her husband, Apostle Rick Ciaramitaro, President of Open Bible Faith Fellowship of Canada, and Senior Pastor of Windsor Christian Fellowship. Cathy is the President of Windsor Life Centre, a home for women who need help to break addictions while in a supportive Christian environment.

Cathy is also known for her dynamic teaching and thought-provoking message on the Cross. Her book, *The Cross: the Power, the Purpose and the Passion* captures the revelation which is her passion, and has sold extensively in Canada.

Cathy is also recognized for her teaching on leadership training and character development, helping believers recognize their strengths and develop the necessary skills for ministry. Admired for her discretion and management ability, she has helped to foster strong staff relationships in the local church and promote healthy personal discipleship.

In her spare time, Cathy enjoys spending time with her six children and sixteen grandchildren.

As an apostolic team, Rick and Cathy oversee more than 500 ministers and leaders worldwide and have preached in

Nepal, India, Vietnam, Russia, the Philippines, Italy, Africa, Latvia, Mexico, and the Caribbean as well as all over North America. Together, Rick and Cathy have over thirty years of experience teaching, nurturing, and feeding the local church.

Another book by Cathy Ciaramitaro

The Cross

Available in both English and Spanish

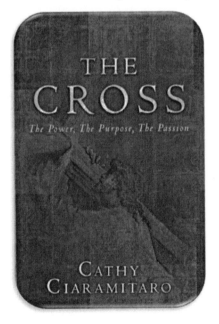

For more information or to purchase
Pastor Cathy's book please visit:
http://www.windsorlifecentre.com/waystohelp.htm

CPSIA information can be obtained at www.ICGtesting.com
Printed in the USA
BVOW082036290113

311907BV00001B/1/P